T0279867

COLORADO
FRONTIERSMEN

COLORADO
FRONTIERSMEN

FORTS, FIGHTS AND LEGACIES

LINDA WOMMACK

THE
History
PRESS

Published by The History Press
Charleston, SC
www.historypress.com

Copyright © 2023 by Linda Wommack
All rights reserved

First published 2023

Manufactured in the United States

ISBN 9781467153652

Library of Congress Control Number: 2022951599

Notice: The information in this book is true and complete to the best of our knowledge. It is offered without guarantee on the part of the author or The History Press. The author and The History Press disclaim all liability in connection with the use of this book.

All rights reserved. No part of this book may be reproduced or transmitted in any form whatsoever without prior written permission from the publisher except in the case of brief quotations embodied in critical articles and reviews.

CONTENTS

INTRODUCTION

Colorado's frontier was a vast open area where men (and women) came to settle and begin new lives.

Before this was possible, frontiersmen, scouts, trappers and traders explored the area, which eventually led to settlement. Men like Kit Carson, who scouted for explorers, including John C. Frémont, also dealt with the Indians in an effort to ford peaceful relations.

The vast frontier was epitomized both in America and Europe by W.F. "Buffalo Bill" Cody. It is fair to say that this frontiersman did more than any other to keep the story of the West alive through his Wild West shows.

Carson and Cody: one man opened the frontier, and the other kept it alive. In between these legendary frontiersmen were myriad others, all legends in their own right.

Charles and William Bent were the first to open a trading post, Bent's Fort, in the frontier West. Both encouraged trade with the Indians; William even married into the Southern Cheyenne tribe. However, Charles, who married a Mexican woman and lived in Taos, was murdered during what has come to be known as the Taos Uprising.

George Bent was the half-Indian son of William Bent. He spent his childhood at Bent's Fort as well as with his mother's tribe. As an adult, he struggled living between the two cultures. It didn't help that as a Confederate soldier, George Bent watched white men kill each other. Then three years later, he watched again as many of his mother's tribe were murdered at Sand Creek.

Jim Beckwourth, a scout and trader who had once been employed at Bent's Fort, was also at Sand Creek. He would later work for peace and live among various Indian tribes.

Two legendary scoutsmen, Mariano Medina and Tom Tobin, made their mark on Colorado's frontier. While Medina opened settlements in the northern region of Colorado, Tobin hunted down the bloody Espinosa Gang. When he cornered them, he cut off their heads, thus ridding the San Luis Valley of the murderous desperados.

As westward migration brought thousands of settlers to the Colorado frontier, forts were established to protect the newcomers. The histories of many of these forts are intertwined with the lives of these frontiersmen. Kit Carson and Jim Beckwourth both attended the historic mountain man rendezvous. Two were held near Fort Davy Crockett, near the Green River in Northwestern Colorado. Carson would spend two hunting seasons working at the fort.

Fort Lyon, an expanded fortress of William Bent's third fort, became the staging point for Colonel John M. Chivington's march to Sand Creek, where several members of Black Kettle's peaceful Cheyenne tribe were murdered. Later, Christopher "Kit" Carson died in the fort's chapel.

Famed frontier scout Thomas Tate Tobin was in charge of the workers who built the adobe fortress known as Fort Garland. Here, Colonel Chivington and his men gathered for the march to Glorieta Pass, the only Civil War battle fought in the West. It was also at Fort Garland where Tom Tobin delivered the heads of the Espinosas to Colonel Sam Tappan. Following the Civil War, Kit Carson served as commander of the fort.

Jim Beckwourth was associated with both Fort Vasquez and Fort Pueblo. He worked at Fort Pueblo for two years and even married one of the local Mexican women.

Fort Sedgwick, originally known as Camp Rankin, was attacked by the Cheyenne dog soldiers, including George Bent. Then they turned their attention to the town of Julesburg, which was attacked and burned no less than three times.

The history of Colorado's early frontier, including the glory and the mistakes of the frontiersmen who paved the way, is recounted within these pages. It all ultimately resulted in the birth of the state of Colorado.

1

THE BENT BROTHERS
AND THEIR HISTORIC FORT

On a warm spring day in 1830, Charles and William Bent stood on a small hill, one of the few in the area, that overlooked the mighty Arkansas River. Here, the Bent brothers constructed the first trading post along the western section of the Santa Fe Trail. For more than fifteen years, Bent's Fort was the dominant structure along the westward route and the hub of all activity. The wagon trains following the Santa Fe Trail regarded the fort as a welcome resting spot. Indians, who watched their land and freedom disappear, traded for supplies at the fort. Conversely, military expeditions pursuing the concept of manifest destiny, guarding and fighting against Indians, used the fort as a point of contact. Of the many traders along the Santa Fe Trail, the Bent brothers proved to be the most adept at working with Indians, as well as the military, in times of conflict.

Silas and Martha Bent of Charleston, Virginia (now West Virginia), were the proud parents of four sons, all of whom would go on to become a part of the American frontier history and directly influence the births of the states of Colorado and New Mexico.

Charles Bent, the eldest of the Bent boys, was born to the affluent Virginia couple on November 11, 1799. William Bent, the second of the Bent brothers, was born in Saint Louis, Missouri, on May 23, 1809. George was born on April 13, 1814, and Robert was born on February 23, 1816.

The Bent brothers grew up in Saint Louis, Missouri, the town later known as the "gateway of the West." It was here that westward expansion began.

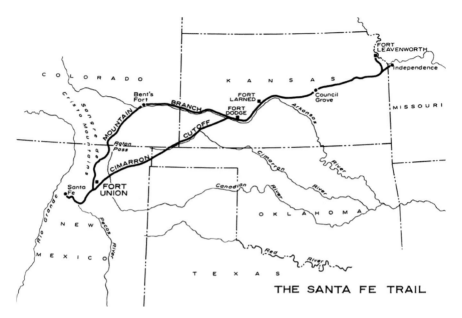

The Santa Fe Trail map. *National Park Service.*

In 1821, entrepreneurs and adventurers sought a way to sell their goods to Mexico. William Becknell is credited with establishing the Santa Fe Trail in November 1821. The 1,200-mile trail stretched from Franklin, Missouri, to Santa Fe, Mexico (now New Mexico). A portion of the trail known as the Mountain Branch followed the Arkansas River, then the border of the United States and Mexico.

Surrounded by this excitement of travel and adventure, Charles Bent joined the Missouri Fur Company, spending considerable time on the upper Missouri River as a trapper. He became skilled with communication and trading with the Indians. Due to his quick wit and learning ability, Bent became a partner in the company in 1823.

In 1827, as a representative of the Missouri Fur Company, Bent and a group of men attended the second annual Mountain Man Rendezvous, which was held at Bear Lake, near the border of today's states of Utah and Idaho.[1] The gathering of traders and Indians was so profitable that Bent soon realized the advantages of trading with the frontiersmen and Indians alike. In 1829, Bent commanded a caravan of wagons loaded with trade goods along the Santa Fe Trail bound for Santa Fe. Again, the trip proved extremely profitable. With such success, Bent formulated a plan to capitalize on the opportunities of the newly opened Santa Fe trade.

Left: William Bent. *Right*: Charles Bent, 1847. *Public domain.*

In 1830, Charles Bent and Ceran Saint Vrain, another Missouri trader among the Plains Indians, established the Bent, Saint Vrain and Company, which became the foundation of a trading empire that covered much of the West, including hundreds of square miles of modern-day Colorado, New Mexico, Arizona, Kansas, Texas and Utah. By this time, Charles's younger brothers George and Robert, at their older brother's invitation, came west and joined in Charles Bent's business venture.

With the help and guidance of their brother-in-law Lilburn Boggs, who was married to Juliannah Bent, the Bent brothers chose a parcel of land along the Santa Fe Trail near the confluence of the Arkansas River and Huerfano Creek in today's southeast Colorado. Boggs, a member of an influential family who had already gained a firm hold on trapping and trading with Indians in the West, was instrumental in helping the Bents acquire the land.

It was here that Bent, Saint Vrain and Company built its first trading post known as Fort William, named after another Bent brother, William, who, by this time, had joined his brothers on the Colorado plains. It was William who planned and supervised the building of the adobe fort. The rectangular stockade was 150 feet long on the north and south sides and 135 feet long on the east and south sides. The walls were 15 feet high and 4 feet thick. The entrance was located on the east side, with two thick plank

Bent's Fort. *Daniel Jenks, 1859; public domain.*

doors providing security. Cannons were placed in the bastions located at the both the northwest and southwest corners. These towers were 10 feet in diameter and 30 feet tall. Cactus plants were planted in the dirt roof to thwart climbers. The central court was open for trading. Rooms were located on the lower and upper levels of the complex. The floors were made of beaten clay. The fort, which could be seen from miles away on the flat land, soon became known as the Citadel of the Plains by travelers along the Santa Fe Trail.

When completed, William became the primary manager of the fort's activities and made successful trading negotiations among the trappers and traders, as well as with the many Indian tribes of the southern plains. Yellow Wolf, the chief of the Cheyenne, became a trustworthy friend of the Bent brothers. He and other leaders affectionately bestowed Cheyenne names on the brothers. Charles was known as Pe-ki-ree, or "White Hat." William was named Schi-vehoe, or "Little White Man." George was called Ho-my-ike, or "Little Beaver," and Robert became known as Otatavi-wee-his, or "Green Bird."

Of the many traders along the Santa Fe Trail, William Bent proved to be quite proficient in adapting to the growing movement of westward migration. As new territories shifted, the Bent, Saint Vrain and Company expanded to meet the demand of territorial commerce. Since their fort was a prominent landmark on the Santa Fe Trail, the Bent brothers, along with Ceran Saint Vrain, were instrumental in the expansion of the United States into Mexico. As such, their trading post was often referred to as Bent's Fort. The name stuck. A year after Bent's Fort opened, the Bent brothers began expanding their commercial enterprise in what would become the largest trading empire in the West. In 1834, William opened a stockade near what is now Pueblo, while Charles built a trading post at Adobe Walls, despite the fact that the territory was disputed by both the United States and Mexico.

Both Charles and William Bent maintained friendly relations with the Indians. In 1835, William Bent married Owl Woman, the daughter of Tall Woman and White Thunder, the keeper of the Cheyenne Sacred Medicine Arrows. Through this intermarriage, the first of several in the Arkansas Valley, a relative peace was maintained between the two cultures for several years. Four children were born to the couple. Mary was born on January 22, 1838, followed by Robert in 1840. George was born on July 7, 1843. Julia was born in 1847. All were born at Bent's Fort.

While William, along with his younger brothers, including eighteen-year-old George and sixteen-year-old Robert, operated the fort, their older brother Charles made regular trips to Santa Fe with wagonloads of trade goods. Charles Bent became so absorbed with the southwestern trade through his travels that he eventually established a permanent home in the Taos Plaza, a small Mexican-Indian town north of Santa Fe.

Also in 1835, Charles Bent met the beautiful widow Maria Ignacia Jaramillo Luna. Maria's husband, Juan Rafael Luna, had died the previous year. Maria's family was well established in the politics of Mexico. Maria's father, Jose Raphael Sena de Luna Sr., was the head of the customs house in Taos, and her mother, Maria Apolonia Jaramillo, was the daughter

Bent's Fort. *National Park Service.*

of Francisco Jaramillo, a successful merchant on the Santa Fe Trail. The Jaramillo family was also related to the Vigil family, who were prominent landowners in northern Mexico and influential in Mexican politics, with Cornelio Vigil being the mayor of Taos. Ceran Saint Vrain, a friend and business partner of Bent, also happened to be a family friend and the godfather of Maria's daughter Rumalda Jaramillo Luna. Following a year of courtship, Charles Bent and Maria Ignacia Jaramillo Luna were married. Maria brought her four-year-old daughter, Rumalda Jaramillo Luna, into the marriage, and Bent later adopted her as his own. Due to the political influence of his new in-laws, Charles also became heavily involved in that town's civic affairs and soon established himself as one of the most prominent, well-respected residents of Taos.

In 1843, Maria's brother Cornelio Vigil and Charles's business partner, Ceran Saint Vrain, applied for a land grant through the Mexican government. These land grants along the Mexican border with the United States were being offered to Mexican citizens in an effort to fortify the area with landowners who were loyal to the Mexican government in the event of war. The tract of land the two men applied for encompassed over two million acres, bounded to the north by the Arkansas River and to the south near today's Colorado–New Mexico border. The land stretched east from the Sangre de Cristo mountain range to the present-day border with Kansas. Perhaps due to the efforts of Vigil's cousin Donaciano Vigil, who served as secretary to Governor Manuel Armijo in Taos, the initial approval for Vigil and Saint Vrain's request was granted. In December 1843, Governor Manuel Armijo traveled north from Taos to personally survey the land and approve the grant, known as the Vigil–Saint Vrain Land Grant.

A year later, Vigil and Saint Vrain "quietly" conveyed one-sixth of the land to Vigil's cousin Donaciano Vigil, another one-sixth to Governor Armijo and a one-sixth portion to Charles Bent. However, by this time, the winds of war between the two countries were strong. In May 1846, Mexican troops crossed the border and fired on U.S. soldiers protecting the southern border. On May 13, 1846, President James Knox Polk went before the U.S. Congress, asking for a declaration of war against Mexico.

Mexican resentment against the American invasion during the war escalated. In July 1846, Charles Bent and Thomas Boggs, who had recently married Bent's stepdaughter, fourteen-year-old Rumalda Luna Jaramillo Bent, were fearful of the escalation of rioting and violence. The men took their wives and family members, including Josefa Carson, the younger sister

Bent's Fort. *Author's photograph.*

of Maria Ignacia Jaramillo Luna Bent and the wife of Christopher "Kit" Carson, to the safety of Bent's Fort, far north of where the war was raging.

The entire country soon learned of the unrest in the Southwest as the Santa Fe de Nuevo Mexican army planned invasions north of the border, with the intention of overtaking Bent's Fort. The U.S. Army was ready.

What the Mexican army did not know—and U.S. Army intelligence did know—was the fact that General Kearny had anticipated such an action. Therefore, in late July 1846, General Stephen Watts Kearny and his troops overtook Bent's Fort, claiming it as the headquarters for Kearny's final onslaught into Mexico. Kearny and his soldiers were treated to a fine reception and welcome.

Samuel and Susan Magoffin were also at Bent's Fort during this time. Samuel and his brother James, operating a trade business along the Santa Fe Trail, had hired Thomas O. Boggs, bringing them to the fort a few days prior.

While staying at the fort, on July 31, 1846, a pregnant nineteen-year-old Susan Magoffin suffered a miscarriage. William Bent helped the grieving Samuel Magoffin bury the child in a spot outside of the fort. Devastated over the loss of her child, Susan Magoffin later wrote in her journal:

*While [I] was miscarrying a child, an Indian woman easily gave birth to
a healthy baby. Within a half hour, the Indian woman walked to the river
to bathe herself and the child.*[2]

For the next few weeks, Charles and Maria Ignacia Bent; their three young
children; their stepdaughter, Rumalda; Rumalda's new husband, Thomas;
and Josefa Carson stayed within the confines of the fort for their safety.

General Stephen Watts Kearny and his army entered Santa Fe on August
18, 1846, and there, they raised the American flag without firing a shot.
When news of Mexico's surrender of the northeastern portion of the
country reached Bent's Fort, Charles Bent's and Thomas Boggs's families
prepared to return to Taos.

Arriving in Taos in early September, Charles Bent found himself in the
middle of the formation of a new territorial government under the auspices
of the United States. Following negotiations between Mexico and the
United States, the boundary between the two countries was moved from the
Arkansas River to the Rio Grande River in Texas.

Bent maintained his influential position among the businessmen of Taos.
He was so influential that in 1846, following General Kearny's successful
military victory, Kearny, on behalf of President K. Polk, appointed Charles
Bent to the office of civilian governor for the new territory of New Mexico.
Later approved by the U.S. Congress, Bent became the first governor of the
newly formed New Mexico Territory.

Governor Charles Bent and the members of the new government,
along with their families, traveled to Santa Fe for a celebration of the
new American territory. On the evening of September 24, 1846, a grand
ball was held at the historic Santa Fe structure known as the Palace of
Governors, the seat of power for the newly created New Mexico Territory.
General Stephen Watts Kearny, acting as a proxy for President James K.
Polk, conveyed the governmental powers to Charles Bent and the other
officials of the new territory. Among the many dignitaries in attendance
were several noted Taos businessmen and women. Attending the festivities
were Samuel and Susan Magoffin, who had resumed their trading business
along the Santa Fe Trail following the loss of their child. Gertrude Barcelo,
the owner of a bordello located near the Palace of Governors, was also in
attendance. Barcelo was known as the former mistress of the last Mexican
governor, Manuel Armijo.[3]

Following the grand gala, Governor Charles Bent returned to Taos, the
seat of the Northern New Mexico Territory. Thus, Bent was able to conduct

government business from his home. For a time after his appointment, it appeared as though the new government would enjoy a peaceful transition. But it was not to be. Shortly after Kearny and most of the army left for California during the Mexican War, the civilian population of Northern New Mexico became extremely unruly. Antagonism over the American military takeover of the area caused both the Indians and Mexicans to cast their alliance with the previous Mexican government rather than supporting the new American authorities. In early October, just a month after taking office, Governor Bent began receiving reports of violence against the new American government and unrest among the people.

Although Governor Bent held out hope for peace in the new territory, the violence continued. During the Christmas season, several arrests were made of those who were leading the plot to overthrow the new government. The Bent family, relieved that such threats had been thwarted, enjoyed a peaceful Christmas celebration with family.

Following the New Year celebrations of 1847 in Santa Fe, Governor Bent and his family traveled north on January 14 to their beloved Taos home on the plaza.

Back in Taos, there was rising resentment among native Mexicans, as well as the local Taos Indians, over the American takeover of their land. Rioting in the streets of Taos resulted in revolting, violence and murder. Before dawn on the cold morning of Friday, January 16, bedlam broke out when a group of Taos Indians, led by Tomasito Romero, stormed into the local jail and freed two of their tribal members, who were being held on petty charges.

By the time Sheriff Stephen Louis Lee arrived at the jail, a large group of angry men had formed a mob. As the group grew larger by the hour, Sheriff Lee was powerless to stop them. Cornelio Vigil, Governor Bent's brother-in-law and a member of the government, tried to reason with the unruly men. Suddenly, a few of the men grabbed Vigil and began beating him. Then others brought out weapons, including knives. When the men started stabbing Vigil repeatedly, others began cutting off his body parts—ears, fingers, legs and arms. Terrified, Sheriff Lee attempted to flee the horrific scene but was caught and killed.

Feeling victorious, Romero led the murderous rioters through Taos to the home of Governor Charles Bent. The family was still asleep in that early hour. However, the family cook, who was preparing the morning meal in the kitchen, heard the approaching mob and alerted the governor. At approximately seven o'clock, as the sun was rising, Bent quickly dressed and went downstairs. Bent was the only man in the residence, as Boggs had accepted the job of courier for the military and Carson was in California with General Kearny. Residing in the Bent home with Maria Ignacia and their children, Alfred, Teresina and Estafina, were Rumalda Bent Boggs and Josefa Jaramillo Carson. While the women and children were safely hidden in an adjoining room, the angry mob shouted and pounded on the front door of the Bent home. As Bent opened the door, hoping to reason with the men, he was shot several times. As Bent fell back inside the home, Maria rushed toward him. A few of the Taos Indians shot arrows inside the house, and one hit Maria Ignacia. Still, Maria Ignacia managed to get to the door, close and bolt it.

In the adjoining room, Josefa and Rumalda used iron spoons and pokers to open a hole through the adobe wall of the house. Incredibly, the two young women were eventually able to make an opening large enough for them to get through. Rumalda and Josefa then helped Alfred, Teresina and Estafina through the opening. By this time, the women could hear the sounds of the frenzied mob and knew they had broken into the house. Just as Maria Ignacia managed to get through the hole in the wall, the maniacal mob stormed into the room.

Rumalda Luna Bent Boggs, who was holding her mortally wounded stepfather, looked up in fear when the mob entered the room. Rumalda watched in horror as Tomasito Romero jerked Bent from Rumalda's clutches and threw him to the floor. What happened next was best related by Rumalda Luna Bent Boggs:

> *He* [Romero] *proceeded to scalp* [Bent] *with a bowstring while he was still yet alive, cutting as cleanly with the tight cord as it could have been done with a knife.*[4]

As Romero and his cohorts began mutilating the lifeless body of Charles Bent, Buenaventura Lobato, one of the instigators of the mob violence, rushed into the Bent home. Disgusted by the bloody remains of Governor Charles Bent, Lobato admonished Romero and the others for killing the governor. Lobato then ordered the men to leave the Bent residence. They did so but not before Romero grabbed the scalp of Charles Bent.

Horrified by the death of Charles Bent and the intimidation by the murderous mob, the Bent family remained in the home in a state of shock. Sometime in the early morning the following day, a few neighbors managed to sneak to the Bent house under the cloak of darkness to deliver food to the women and children.

Bent's Fort, interior. *Author's photograph.*

James P. Beckwourth, a longtime friend and occasional employee of the Bent brothers, had witnessed the murder and rode through the night and for half a day to Bent's Fort with the grim news. But word of mouth traveled faster; Bent family member and frontiersman Charles Autobees had already broken the devastating news to the Bent brothers. William and his younger brother George executed a secret retrieval of Charles's body, which was necessary given the violent climate of the area. Charles Bent was secretly buried near a wall at Bent's Fort, next to the grave of his youngest brother, Robert, who was also murdered on October 20, 1841, scalped by Comanche Indians along the Santa Fe Trail. Several years later, the body of Charles Bent was returned to Santa Fe and given an honorable burial.[5] After two days of murderous rampaging, the violence was finally over. A wounded Maria Ignacia Bent, her three children and Rumalda and Josefa finally felt safe enough to leave their home. The women and children joined several other terrified Taos citizens who were offered sanctuary at the fortified home of Padre Antonio José Martínez.

In July 1847, William, still grieving over the murder of his brother, suffered another loss. Owl Woman died from complications in childbirth. Her sister

Yellow Woman took charge of Owl Woman's body. After washing the body, she carefully dressed her deceased sister in her finest beaded deerskin dress. In the Cheyenne custom, Owl Woman's body was then carried to the bank of the Arkansas River. There, the body was placed on a scaffold, which was then lifted into a notch of a cottonwood tree, a Cheyenne spiritual act. Following the Cheyenne burial ceremony, Yellow Woman presented Owl Woman's baby girl to William. Though he was grieving, it was the first time he saw his fourth child. William named her Julia after his sister.

Meanwhile, William's younger brother, George, had become an instrumental force in the Bent, Saint Vrain and Company, working for several years with his brothers, handling and expanding their business enterprise. Like his older brother Charles, George also divided his time between Bent's Fort and a home in Taos. After Charles's murder, George was appointed foreman of the grand jury, hearing testimony regarding the events that took his brother's life. George Bent died suddenly of a fever at Bent's Fort on October 23, 1847, less than a year after the death of Charles. Within nine months in 1847, William Bent suffered the deaths of two brothers and his beloved wife.

In 1849, an outbreak of cholera killed a large percentage of the Southern Cheyenne and Comanche tribes in the region. Because of the health epidemic, Bent's Fort was deserted. William, who had recently married Owl Woman's sister Yellow Woman, took his new wife and infant son, Charles, and his three young children, Mary, Robert and George, to the Big Timbers area, some twenty miles down river along the Arkansas River.

Perhaps due to the cholera outbreak—or his grief of losing so many loved ones—William attempted to sell the stockade to the U.S. government. After a period of negotiation, the government finally declined to purchase the fort. Out of frustration, William Bent set fire to explosives in the gunpowder room of the fort. Lighting the fuse, he ran from the fort and watched as the explosion blasted the infamous stockade to ruins. With this act, the Citadel of the Plains was no more, and an important era of Colorado's frontier came to an end.

With a caravan of wagons loaded with trade goods, William traveled fifteen miles along the river to join Yellow Woman and her people at Big Timbers. There, for the next few years, William traded with the friendly Cheyenne and Arapaho tribes.

In 1853, William built a new fort, commonly known as Bent's New Fort. Located in the Big Timbers of the Santa Fe Trail, this new stockade was constructed on elevated ground above the river. While the position provided a commanding view from all directions, it could be accessed from only one direction, an added benefit for security purposes. As such, William felt it was in a better location than his previous fort had been. The new fort was built of local stone, with walls that were ten feet high. Cannons were placed on each corner of its flat roof. There were twelve rooms around the central court, where trading took place.

William built a wooden lodge for his family. There, the children—twelve-year-old Robert, ten-year-old George, five-year-old Julia and two-year-old Charles—played with the Indian children. Fourteen-year-old Mary worked with her stepmother in the duties required of Cheyenne women. For the next few years, peace and harmony existed for the Bent children, who lived in two cultural worlds. Following the discovery of gold in the Colorado Rocky Mountains in 1859, a new onslaught of travelers and gold seekers moved along the Santa Fe Trail, heading west toward prosperity and fortune. For the otherwise peaceful Indian tribes in the region, the encroachment of such a large population caused tension among the traders and Indians at Bent's Fort. William Bent worked to establish peace between the two cultures and advocated for a peaceful solution. He sent a strong letter to Superintendent of Indian Affairs A.M. Robinson, requesting a commission to come west to offer a treaty defining the Indians' rights "before they cause a great deal of trouble." Robinson, who knew the ways of Washington, D.C., knew this was an unreasonable request. Yet he respected William Bent and sent his own missive to Washington, D.C., asking that William Bent be appointed the Indian agent of the Arkansas Territory. On April 27, 1859, the commission was approved and signed by President James Buchanan.

Clearly, Little White Man, as the Cheyenne called William, was advocating on behalf of his wife's and children's people. In mid-July, William and his oldest son, Robert, traveled to the junction of the South Platte River and Beaver Creek to meet with the Cheyenne. In his first report to his superior, Superintendent Robinson, Bent wrote:

> *The Cheyans* [sic] *and Arapahos have took my advice to them. I am proud to say they have behaved themselves exceedingly well. Theair* [sic] *will be no trouble settling them down and start farming. They tell me they have passed theair laws among themselves that they will do anything I may advize* [sic]. *After I deliver the Indians theair goods, I intend to have a conversation with the Kioways and Commanches* [sic]. *I suppose that they will be purtay* [sic] *saucy—but as I have bin* [sic] *appointed agent, I feel*

it my duty to see all of the Indians under my agency—if they scalp me. You must excuse my bad spelling, as I have bin [sic] so long in the Wild Waste [sic], I have almost forgotton how to spell.[6]

In late July, Bent returned to Bent's New Fort, where he received nearly three thousand members of the Arapaho, Apache and Cheyenne tribes. There at his stone fort, Bent distributed the government's allotment of annuities. During this time, Major John Sedgwick arrived at the fort with three hostages whom he captured at Kiowa chief Satanta's village. The hostages were Satanta's wife and two children. Somehow, either due to inadequate guarding of the hostages or Bent's allowing, the hostages escaped. That fall, Sedgwick received orders from the War Department to build a new military post at Big Timbers. Whether Sedgwick acted in retaliation for the hostage escape at Bent's New Fort is unknown. However, after talks with Bent, it was agreed that Bent was willing to sell his establishment. Sedgwick sent a strong letter to the assistant adjutant general, suggesting the government buy Bent's New Fort.

On September 9, 1860, Bent signed a temporary lease with Lieutenant James B. McIntyre, the regimental quartermaster. Ten days later, Bent resigned as Indian agent and recommended Albert Gallatin Boone as his replacement. Bent moved his family to the mouth of Purgatory Creek, near the Purgatoire River, where he kept busy enlarging a trading post he had built three years previously. The square wooden fortress was one foot thick on all sides. The walls were fifteen feet high. Heavy square-hewn log beams were laid across the walls and attached with wooden pins. Inside, the rooms were arranged around the open central court. The Bent family's quarters were located on the north end, and warehouses were located on the south end. A large gate that could accommodate freight wagons was built into the southern wall. Robert helped his father with the construction, and soon, Mary, along with her husband and new baby, joined the family. William's younger sons, George and Charley, were attending school in Westport, Missouri, at the time.

Seven months later, in April 1861, the Civil War broke out between the states. That summer, George Bent enlisted with the Confederate army, and Charley would soon follow. During the war, William Bent remained loyal to the Union. He also made a lucrative living by hauling freight wagons between the Purgatoire River stockade and the markets in Taos, New Mexico.

Meanwhile, the government had revoked Bent's signed lease of Bent's New Fort. Soldiers were assigned to the fort, and it was fortified and enlarged. The military fort was renamed Fort Wise, after Henry Alexander Wise, the governor of Virginia. However, the name was changed in August 1861 to Fort Lyon. The name change was done in honor of General Nathaniel Lyon, the first Union general killed in the Civil War. His death occurred at the Battle of Wilson's Creek, near Springfield, Missouri, on August 10, 1861.

Ironically, just eighty miles southwest of Wilson's Creek, on March 6, 1862, the Battle of Pea Ridge was launched in Northwest Arkansas. George Bent was present and fought in the battle. Following the Confederate defeat, George was captured by the Union army in Corinth, Arkansas, in October 1862. George and the other prisoners were sent to a prison in Missouri. As luck would have it, George's older brother Robert happened to be in Saint Louis at the time. When word of his brother's imprisonment reached him, Robert intervened. Because Robert was the son of the respected William Bent, the military officers released George into his care, with the stipulation that Robert take his brother back west. In early 1863, Robert and George returned to their father's stockade at Purgatoire River. Shortly after this reunion, Charley arrived at the Bent family compound. Both had seen enough of the white man's war. Within a few weeks, George and Charley rode off to join the Cheyenne camp. The following summer, William's youngest daughter, Julia, married Edward Guerrier, the half-Indian son of trapper William Guerrier. Shortly after the wedding, the couple also left for the Cheyenne camp. Meanwhile, William worked closely with Major Edward Wynkoop, the commander of Fort Lyon, to come up with a peaceful solution with the Arapaho and Cheyenne. However, Territorial Governor John Evans thwarted the peaceful negotiations that William Bent and Commander Wynkoop had started. On June 16, 1864, Evans issued an executive order, requiring all citizens to report all reliable information regarding "reference to Indians" immediately.

Then, just ten days later, Evans sent a peace proposal to the Indian tribes of the Colorado Territory. Undoubtedly, it was extended because Evans had been denied his requests for military reinforcements due to the raging Civil War in the East. Evans's proposal, printed in the *Rocky Mountain News* issue of June 27, 1864, was also sent to all the Indian agents in the territory.

Major S.E. Colley, the Indian agent at Fort Lyon, asked William Bent to distribute copies of the peace proposal to the many Indian camps in the Arkansas Valley. Bent enlisted the help of interpreter John Smith and Cheyenne chief One-Eye to deliver the proposal to camps north of the Arkansas River, while Bent traveled alone to the camps south of the river.

Above, left: John Evans was complicit in the Sand Creek debacle. *Denver Public Library.*

Above, right: Edward Wynkoop worked for peace with Black Kettle. *Denver Public Library.*

Right: Colonel John M. Chivington ordered his Colorado volunteers to strike at a peaceful Indian village along Sand Creek in Colorado. *Denver Public Library.*

When the Cheyenne, led by Black Kettle, arrived at Fort Lyon, William was pleased to find that his sons George and Charley were with them. However, while Bent had been away from the fort, a change in personnel had occurred.

On November 5, 1864, Major Scott J. Anthony had arrived at Fort Lyon from Fort Leavenworth, carrying written orders signed by General Samuel R. Curtis, commander of military operations in the West. The general's order was simple and direct: by Special Order No. 13, Major Wynkoop had been relieved of his command of Fort Lyon and replaced by Major Anthony.[7]

Both the Arapaho and Cheyenne tribes had great faith and trust in the peaceful intentions of Major Wynkoop. Conversely, they did not trust this new commander. Major Anthony's "dark disposition" and physical appearance alarmed the Indians. They referred to him as the "red-eyed chief." Anthony assured the Indians that he believed in Wynkoop's policy. Therefore, Anthony immediately suggested that Black Kettle and Left Hand move their people to Sand Creek, approximately forty miles northeast of Fort Lyon. Anthony assured them that they would be safe there and under the military's protection. A few days later, Left Hand and Black Kettle moved their lodges to Sand Creek.

However, Colonel John M. Chivington had an entirely different plan. Chivington had led his newly created "100 day volunteers" southeast for ten days in sub-zero temperatures and through deep snow. Early in the morning of Monday, November 28, Chivington ordered a group of soldiers from the Colorado Third, under Lieutenant Joseph Graham, to cross the Arkansas River and move toward William Bent's ranch along Purgatoire River. Graham's additional order was to "put the place under guard, allowing no one to leave." The military siege of the Bent property was significant in Chivington's secrecy of his military campaign, as William Bent was the father of half-Indian sons whom he believed consorted with the enemy.

At the Bent ranch, the family was ordered inside the home, and guards were placed at all the doors. The Bent family was told that anyone who attempted to escape would be shot. Robert Bent, the eldest son of William, was ordered to aid Jim Beckwourth in guiding the soldiers to the Cheyenne camp. Ironically, this was the village of his mother's people, where his brother George and three younger half sisters were living. Forced into such a position, what went through Robert Bent's mind is anyone's guess.

Chivington and his volunteer troops arrived at Sand Creek in the dark hours of the early morning of Tuesday, November 29, 1864. The troops, nearly seven hundred strong, were strategically positioned on three sides of the Cheyenne village. Included in their artillery were four twelve-pound mountain howitzers. Camped in the ravine near the creek were some six hundred Indians, primarily women and children, along with Chiefs Little Raven, White Antelope, Left Hand and Black Kettle. William Bent's adult children, George, Charley and Julia Bent Guerrier, were also there. At dawn, Chivington ordered the attack on the Indian encampment. Hearing the first shots, George Bent rushed from his tipi and watched in horror as White Antelope was shot down in a single round of fire. Robert Bent was nearby, watching the horror unfold. He, too, watched as White Antelope, showing signs of peace, was shot by the soldiers.

The soldiers advanced and shot John Smith. Horribly frightened and confused, several elderly men ran for the shelter of a lodge, where John Smith's son Jack, Charley Bent and his brother-in-law, Ed Guerrier, were hiding.

George Bent grabbed his weapons and ran for the bluffs along the west side of Sand Creek. Ed Guerrier was able to run north to safety. Ed was picked up by his cousin, one of White Antelope's daughters, who had captured a few horses. During the six-hour battle, George Bent received a bullet wound to the hip but managed to escape north of the area. When the fighting ended and the soldiers were destroying what was left of the camp, Robert Bent was released from his forced captivity by Chivington's troops. While the horrific Sand Creek Massacre was over, it would haunt William Bent's children for the rest of their lives.

Robert Bent returned to his father's trading post at Purgatoire River, where he worked with his father and tried to put the tragedy behind him as best he could. By this time, William's oldest daughter, Mary, and her husband, Territorial Judge R.M. Moore, were also living at Purgatoire River.

Robert's younger brother George, who was wounded in the massacre, recovered at the Fort Lyon Hospital, where his father, William, watched over him. When he was well enough, George returned to the Cheyenne people and joined the dog soldiers, with whom he fought furiously against the white man, leading raids and causing terror across the eastern plains.

Charley Bent never forgot the forced march and also joined the Cheyenne dog soldiers in war against the white settlers. His hatred for the white man was so strong that, in time, he began to hate his father, William. There was one white person whom Charley harbored no resentment for: his older sister Mary. When he could, Charley would approach the Bent family compound to see Mary. If William was not present, it was deemed safe, and Mary would place a lantern in the window. So was the routine one night in 1867, when

New Bent's Fort ruins. *Photograph by John Stanton, Fortwiki (CC BY-SA 3.0).*

Mary saw her brother crouching in the ditch near the house. After leaving the house to greet her brother, she invited him inside. Charley uncocked his gun, lowered it and declined the invitation, saying he wanted to kill the "old man." With that, Charley left. When William learned of the attempt on his life by his own son, he disowned him. A year later, Charley Bent was killed by bullet to his back.

William Bent continued to negotiate for peace between the white man and the Indians following his testimony in the military inquiries regarding the actions of Colonel Chivington at the Sand Creek Massacre.

William Bent died of pneumonia in 1869. Until his death, he was still trading and seeking peace between the Indians and the encroaching white men. He was buried in the Las Animas Cemetery in the seat of Bent County, named for the great frontiersman.

For over forty years, William Bent was known as the "Peace Keeper" among the Native Americans. His expansive trading empire was the largest in western America. For more than fifteen years, Bent's Fort was the dominant structure in the West, the hub of all activity. Military expeditions pursued the concept of manifest destiny, an important role in the expansion of the western frontier. All the while, the Bent brothers welcomed Indian trade and became advocates for the Native Americans. William Bent's legacy continues to this day.

On June 3, 1960, the realization of much hard work by local, state and national activists came to fruition when President Dwight D. Eisenhower designated Bent's Old Fort a National Historic Site. After nearly ten years of painstaking archaeology, in 1976, the centennial year for the State of Colorado, the National Park Service began the reconstruction of Bent's Old Fort. The 1846 drawings of Lieutenant James A. Abert, a topographical engineer, were vital in rebuilding the adobe fort on its original foundation. The grass-reinforced adobe fort was built by the U.S. Department of Interior and the National Park Service. The replica fort at Bent's Old Fort National Historic Site is located fourteen miles from Las Animas on Colorado Highway 194. It is now a national tourist site staffed by National Park Service volunteers in period costume.

2

FORT DAVY CROCKETT

FUR TRAPPERS AND INDIAN TRADING

In 1836, mountain men William Craig, Previtt Sinclair and Philip Thompson built a fort at Brown's Hole, where Vermillion Creek merges with the Green River. Brown's Hole is best described as a valley that is nearly fifty miles long, stretching from Colorado's northwestern Moffat County to the eastern border of Utah's Daggett County. It is a beautiful valley sitting between mountains and rock cliffs and was a favorite wintering place for Indians, trappers and traders. After news of the fall of the Alamo and the death of Davy Crockett reached the mountains, the owners of the fort at Brown's Hole named it after the fallen hero. Located on the north shore of the Green River, approximately ten miles above the Gates of Lodore in the valley of Brown's Hole, Fort Davy Crockett became the social center of the Rocky Mountains. Scoutsmen, hunters and trappers were hired at the fort. The renowned frontiersman Christopher "Kit" Carson spent two years hunting wild game at the fort. Business at the fort included trading with Indians and trappers who were working in the region.

Described as a "hollow square," Fort Davy Crockett was built of logs and had a dirt roof and dirt floor, which quickly became a muddy mess in foul weather. Thus, it soon became a squalid, insect-infested place. A German traveler, Frederick A. Wislizenus, stayed at the fort in 1839 and complained he couldn't get an hour's rest there because of the mosquitoes. He later described the fort:

> *It is a low one-story building constructed of wood and clay, with three connecting wings and no enclosure. The whole establishment appeared*

somewhat poverty-stricken, for which reason it is also known to the trappers by the name of Fort Misery.[8]

Another traveler, T.J. Farnham, who stayed at the fort in 1839, described it as "a square of one-story log cabins with roofs and floors of mud. It was the meanest fort in the West."

In the summer of 1839, thousands of trappers and over 1,500 Indians gathered for the annual mountain man rendezvous near the Green River and Horse Creek in today's Wyoming. The Rocky Mountain fur trade was in decline by the late 1830s, but it remained alive and well on the banks of the Green River at Fort Davy Crockett. Since 1835, the rendezvous had been held in this area, with many of the participants spending the winter in nearby Brown's Hole. With more accessible regions trapped out, Brown's Hole offered some of the best beaver trapping in the Green River, which flowed through a portion of the region. Thus, Fort Davy Crockett enjoyed a brief period as host of the mountain men and Indians during the summer rendezvous.

Following the annual mountain man rendezvous of 1840, which was the last rendezvous, Fort Davy Crockett again became the center of entertainment for hundreds of trappers, traders and Indians. Among those who stayed in Brown's Hole that historic year were Jim Beckwourth, Kit Carson, Joe Walker, Jim Baker and Joe Meek, his brother-in-law, Robert "Doc" Newell and their wives, sisters of the Nez Perce tribe.

Unfortunately, it was at Fort Davy Crockett that an incident of horse stealing by the attending Indians caused a split in the once-peaceful relationship between the mountain men and the Indians. Such an act had never before happened during the rendezvous. Doc Newell was so shocked that he declared, "Such a thing has never been known till late."

An eyewitness to subsequent events, E. Willard Smith, wrote of the event in his journal:

On the evening of November 1, 1840, a party of Sioux who had tracked a band of Snake Indians, discovered Brown's Hole and its secret. The war party located the horse herd and made off with 150 head.[9]

Several of the mountain men went after the Indians and horses. Kit Carson, Joe Meek and Doc Newell were among the group of twenty-five men led by famed frontiersman Joseph Reddeford Walker. They tracked the renegades over the ice-covered Green River to the vicinity of Fort Uintah

The Green River at the Gates of Lodore in Brown's Park, Colorado. *Denver Public Library.*

in the Utah area, and there, they surrounded their camp. While Walker and the other mountain men had no desire to fight the Sioux Indians, they were determined to get their horses back. The leader of this band of Sioux recognized Walker and realized that the white men were serious. The horses were surrendered to Walker. Thus, a bloody fight was avoided.

31

This marker indicates the site of Fort Davy Crockett in today's Moffat County. *Public domain.*

The raid caused considerable consternation at Fort Davy Crockett. The act of horse theft in spite of otherwise friendly encounters contributed to the demoralized attitude of the mountain men who were staying at the fort in the winter of 1840. The beavers were nearly played out, and what could be trapped brought low prices due to a lack of demand. It was the end of the American fur trading enterprise. By early summer 1841, the fort was abandoned, as the trappers, traders and even the Indians left the Brown's Hole area. Fort Davy Crockett, poorly built by all accounts, did not fare well in the region's inclement weather. Thus, the fort quickly fell to ruin. The historic fort, so prominent as a trading post during the twilight of the nation's fur trading era, became a thing of the past. Not long after its abandonment, the fort was destroying by fire, most likely by Utes who began raiding in the area in 1845. This band of Ute warriors had also burned Fort Uintah, near the confluence of the Green, Duchesne and White Rivers that same year.

In 1975, Glade Ross, a ranger with the Bureau of Land Management based at the Lodore Station of Dinosaur National Monument, uncovered evidence of the historic fort on the north shore of the Green River in Brown's Hole, now known as Brown's Park, Colorado. On a steep cutbank of the river, two feet below the surface, Ross spotted a definitive line of charcoal. A team of archaeologists from Denver examined the site and found the remains of a log wall that stretched nearly 140 feet. Also uncovered were beads, several five-hole buttons, musket balls, melted lead, a percussion cap, gun flints, a musket hammer and a brass gun forestock, possibly from a Hawken rifle.

Today, a historical marker represents the site of Fort Davy Crockett, which is in the National Register of Historic Places and protected by the National Wildlife Service.

3

FAMED FRONTIERSMAN CHRISTOPHER "KIT" CARSON

Christopher Houston "Kit" Carson, while a complex individual, undoubtedly left his mark in the annals of the history of the American West. He was a man of extraordinary strengths and significant weaknesses. A restless adventurer, he was also devoted to his family. Despite his independent spirit, he was an an obedient soldier who was loyal to his superiors.

Kit Carson was born in Madison County, Kentucky, on December 24, 1809, to Lindsey and Rebecca Robinson Carson. Lindsey Carson fought in the American Revolutionary War from 1775 to 1783. In 1796, he married Rebecca Robinson. When Christopher was born, he was the sixth of ten children born to the couple. In 1811, the Carson family moved to Franklin Township, Howard County, Missouri, in an area known as Boone's Lick, where they engaged in farming.[10] In October 1815, an Indian uprising occurred in the area. Sixty-year-old Lindsey Carson joined a small group to fight the Indians. During a skirmish, Carson was shot in the hand and lost two fingers. For the next several years, the Indians were a constant threat.

Young Carson attended public school when he could, but he was often needed to help with the farming duties at home. His younger sister could not say "Christopher," so she called him "Kit," and the name stuck.[11] Carson did well with arithmetic but never learned to read or write. Curiously, he had a knack for learning languages and picked up Indian dialects with ease. At home, Carson became quite proficient with a shotgun and a rifle, often providing meat for the family. Tragically, in September 1818, Lindsey Carson was killed by a falling tree branch while clearing land by fire. Four years later, Carson's mother married Joseph Martin.

When Kit was fourteen, his stepfather apprenticed him to a saddlemaker in Old Franklin. This was the site where most of the fur trading with Santa Fe, New Mexico, occurred, and it was the starting point of the Santa Fe Trail. Carson later revealed in his autobiography his dislike of the apprenticeship.

Kit Carson first worked at Fort Davy Crockett before his famous escapades across Colorado's vast frontier. *Denver Public Library.*

> *For fifteen years I lived in Missouri, and during that time I dwelt in Howard County. I was apprenticed to David Workman to learn the saddler's trade, and remained with him two years. The business did not suit me and, having heard so many tales of life in the mountains of the West, I concluded to leave him. He was a good man, but taking into consideration that if I remained with him and served my apprenticeship, I would have to pass my life in labor. That was distasteful to me, and being anxious to travel for the purpose of seeing different countries, I concluded to join the first party that started for the Rocky Mountains. In August 1826, I had the good fortune to hear of one bound for that country. I made application to join this party, and was accepted without any difficulty.*

The scouting party Carson joined was led by Ewing Young. Because of his age, Carson's duties were limited to cooking for the men and feeding the animals. Carson later said, "I obtained employment as a cook with Mr. Ewing Young, my board being the remuneration." For the next several years, Carson remained with Young. The two scouted in the area of today's New Mexico, spending considerable time in Taos. Carson quickly learned to communicate with the Native Americans in several languages, including Apache, Arapaho, Blackfoot, Cheyenne, Comanche, Crow, Navajo, Shoshone, Paiute and Ute, as well as a sign language used among western tribes.

In August 1829, Carson, Young and a group of trappers and traders left Taos to pursue their trade farther west. For the next two years, the group trapped for beaver along the streams from what would become Arizona to California. Carson gained invaluable experience as a frontier trapper, and this served him well for the rest of his life. It was also during this time that Carson quickly learned French, having spent so much time with French trappers. He also became fluent in Spanish and was able to interpret in various negotiations. By 1834, Carson was trapping with Jim Bridger and Thomas Fitzpatrick in the Wind River Mountain Range of Wyoming. He got into fights with the Shoshone and Blackfeet and nearly lost his life when a bullet from a Blackfoot warrior grazed his neck.

The following year, Carson attended the annual mountain man rendezvous in Wyoming's Green River Valley.

It was here that Carson became enamored with a young northern Arapaho maiden by the name of Waa-nibe, whom he had met at the rendezvous the previous summer. Again, Carson's raw courage and quick wit served him well. It happened in a duel of honor. A French-Canadian trapper known only as Shunar also had designs on the same young Arapaho woman. Shunar was described as an overweight loudmouth bully.

Through his research, historian Marc Simmons revealed that the French-Canadian trapper was actually Joseph Chouinard. In any case, one day during the rendezvous, Chouinard chose to spend the day drinking and harassing several men within his group of trappers. By late afternoon, he had instigated three fights, beating his targeted opponents severely. Incredibly, throughout the day, no one challenged the drunken bully. As Chouinard made his way to the American trappers' camp, he let it be known to all that he meant to "beat the Americans like children."

With that remark, Chouinard abruptly turned and left the area. As Carson watched Chouinard mount his horse, Carson mounted his. As Chouinard rode into the camp, Carson's horse galloped to meet him. With their horses touching, Carson asked, "Am I the one you're fixin' to shoot?" At that same instant, Chouinard pulled his shotgun from its holder. Carson remained calm. As soon as Chouinard leveled his gun at Carson, Carson fired his pistol. Eyewitnesses said that the shots from the two men were so close together that they thought only one shot was fired. Carson's shot hit Chouinard in his shooting arm, while Chouinard's shot missed Carson.

This was one of many incidents in which Carson's keen instincts and ability to remain calm under fire served him well. He would not only have a successful military career, but he would also become a legendary frontiersman.

One of Carson's closest friends, Smith H. Simpson, claimed that Carson told him "the duel was over this squaw, and the Frenchman got mad. The

Kit Carson's famed horseback duel. *Charlie M. Russell, engraving; public domain.*

Frenchman was the only man he ever killed that he was pleased with." In any event, shortly after the 1835 rendezvous, twenty-five-year-old Kit Carson took the northern Arapaho maiden Waa-nibe as his wife. Carson recounted, "In September, camp was broken, and we divided into parties of convenient size and started on our fall hunt."

Carson joined a small party associated with the Hudson's Bay Fur Company. That summer, he and Waa-nibe attended the annual rendezvous, again at the confluence of Green River and Horse Creek. In the spring of 1837, Waa-nibe gave birth to a baby girl. Carson named her Adeline after a family member of his in Missouri. In August that year, Carson and his young family attended the rendezvous, again held at Green River. For the next year, Carson remained in the area, trapping with many of his old friends. In 1838, the annual rendezvous was held on the plains, near the Wind and Popo Agie Rivers in today's Wyoming. By this time, beavers were becoming extremely scarce. At the same time, the demand for beaver pelts had fallen. As it was apparent that the western fur trade was fading, the attendance at the rendezvous was nearly half of what it had been in past years. This was the primary topic of discussion among the trappers and traders who did attend. Carson, having had many talks with his fellow trappers, chose to take a different career path. At the conclusion of the rendezvous, Carson took his family southwest to Brown's Hole.

The area of Brown's Hole, today's northwestern corner of Colorado, was an isolated valley surrounded by rugged terrain to the north, east and west. Fort Davy Crockett, located on the northwestern shore of the Green River, became the new social center for trappers, traders and Ute Indians in the Rocky Mountains. It was here, on September 1, 1838, that Carson and a group of men rode into the fort.

For the next two years, Carson worked as a scout and hunter at Fort Davy Crockett. While at the fort, in the spring of 1840, Waa-nibe gave birth to her second child. Sadly, Waa-nibe died shortly after giving birth. Most historians believe Waa-nibe died from puerperal fever, also known as childbed fever. It was an infection that occurred shortly after childbirth and was not uncommon in the era.[12] For the rest of his life, Carson rarely spoke of Waa-nibe.

In the summer of that tragic year, Carson left his two daughters at Fort Davy Crockett and attended the annual rendezvous. Again held on the shores of Green River, it was the last of the historic mountain man rendezvous ever held. During 1841, Carson continued to hunt wild game for the fort, which provided an income and help with his daughters. In the fall, Carson and a group of men, including the legendary trapper "Old Bill" Williams, set out for Bent's Fort along the Arkansas River in the southeastern plains of Colorado.

By September 1841, Carson was in the employ of Charles and William Bent. While Carson worked for the Bent brothers, his daughters were cared for by Charlotte Green, the fort's cook. It was during his time at Bent's Fort that Carson married a Cheyenne girl, Making Out Road. The couple lived together in their own tipi at the fort for nearly a year. For whatever reason—and Carson never said—Making Out Road divorced him Cheyenne style, placing his personal possessions outside of the tipi.

Apparently undaunted—as Carson would later say the marriage was a mistake—Carson accompanied a group of men who were taking supplies to Charles Bent's store in Taos. It was the first time since 1826 that Carson had returned to the frontier town.

Carson spent many evenings socializing at the home of Charles and Maria Ignacia Bent. It was here that Carson became acquainted with Maria Josefa Jaramillo, the younger half sister of Maria Ignacia Bent. The two courted for a time. When Carson asked Josefa's father, Don Francisco Jaramillo, for his daughter's hand in marriage, Carson was told he must convert to Catholicism. On January 28, 1842, Carson was baptized in Our Lady of Guadalupe Church at Taos. Padre Antonio José Martínez performed the ceremony.

In an effort to provide the best education possible for his daughter Adeline, Carson decided to take her to relatives in Missouri. William Bent and his partner Ceran Saint Vrain entrusted Carson to lead a caravan of wagons loaded with the winter's hides and other trade goods to the market trading center of Saint Louis, Missouri.

Eager to return to Bent's Fort, Carson booked passage on a steamship on the Missouri River. It would was a decision that would change his life and elevate his frontier legacy. Meanwhile, Carson had evidently left his three-year-old daughter in the care of Maria Ignacia Luna Bent, as the details of her death are revealed in Bent family letters. Tragically, the toddler fell into a large kettle of boiling soap. When Carson returned to Bent's Fort, he was devastated by the news of the death of his younger daughter. In typical Carson fashion, he never mentioned her again—even her name has been lost in the history of Carson's life. Finally, with the arrival of Frémont and his men, Carson seized on the opportunity of adventure in the unknown West.

Lieutenant John Charles Frémont, with the U.S. Topographical Engineers, had been commissioned to lead an expedition of men to explore upper Platte River into the Rocky Mountains. The group of twenty-one men included Lucien Maxwell as the hunter, Charles Preuss as the topographer and Carson as the chief scout. The expedition traversed the rugged Rocky Mountains to South Pass in today's state of Wyoming. With this, the first of Frémont's four expeditions was completed. The ease of travel through the mountain range was due in no small part to Carson's ability as a scout, as Frémont noted in his government report.

During the return trip east, when the group reached Fort Laramie on August 31, 1842, Carson, as he later stated, "quit the employ of Frémont. I went to Bent's Fort." Shortly after Carson arrived at Bent's Fort in mid-January 1843, he made preparations for travel to Taos.

On Monday, February 6, 1843, thirty-three-year-old Christopher "Kit" Carson and fourteen-year-old Maria Josefa Jaramillo were married in Our Lady of Guadalupe Church at Taos. Padre Antonio José Martínez performed the ceremony. With the money Carson had earned from the Frémont expedition, he purchased an 1825 four-room adobe home for his new bride.

In his dictated autobiography, for the first time, Carson mentioned his marriage:

> *In February of same year* [1843] *got married to Senorita Josefa Jaramilla* [sic], *a daughter of Don Francisco Jaramilla. I remained in Taos till April, then worked with Bent and Saint Vrain.*

Kit Carson scouted for John C. Fremont on his famous discovery expeditions. *Public domain.*

Once again, Carson worked as a hunter for the Bent brothers. That summer, the Bents paid Carson $300 to deliver a message to the governor of New Mexico Manuel Armijo, asking for military protection along the Santa Fe Trail. Mexican uprisings along the trail had caused harassment among the travelers and even theft in many cases. It was a foreshadowing of the cultural unrest brewing in the region.

Returning to Bent's Fort in May 1843, Carson received a message from Frémont, who was camped some seventy miles upriver along the Arkansas River. While Frémont continued with his westward travel up the Arkansas River, Carson returned to Bent's Fort, where he assembled a group of able mountain men to join Frémont's second exploration. Carson also procured additional horses and mules from the fort for the trip. Carson later said, "I was well received at the fort and furnished all that I required." Before Carson left to join Frémont, he was able to send a message to Josefa of his impending departure for the West. By September, Carson had joined Frémont's expedition. He recalled, "[We] delivered flour and a few other articles of light provision, sufficient for two or three days—a scanty but very acceptable supply."

Until then, Frémont's chief guide was Thomas Fitzpatrick, one of the best trackers in the West. Upon Carson's arrival, Fitzpatrick relinquished his chief guide duties to his old friend Kit Carson. Now with an able team of scouts, sixty-seven horses and mules, ammunition and arms, including a bronze mountain howitzer, Frémont set out to explore and map the Oregon Trail from Missouri to Fort Vancouver.

After crossing South Pass, Frémont followed a southern route along the Oregon Trail. Early snowstorms slowed the expedition, and the group's provisions began to run low. Rather than face death from cold and starvation, Frémont made the hasty decision to turn west and cross the Sierra Nevadas to Sutter's Fort in California. It was now mid-December, and the mountain range was covered with deep snow. The group met a band of Washoe Indians, who discouraged Frémont from crossing the Sierra Nevada

Mountain Range. Carson translated the Washoe leader's warning as, "Rock upon rock, snow upon snow."

Disregarding the warning, Frémont pushed on. By the end of January 1844, the expedition had reached a river later known as Carson River. Here, the group set camp, soon dubbed "Long Camp"—for good reason. Despite the harsh conditions Preuss so adequately described, Carson was able to lead the Frémont party out of the snowy mountain range, and they arrived at Sutter's Fort in March 1844. After a month's stay at the fort, Carson led the group east through the San Joaquin Valley and over Walker Pass. From there, the Frémont party made their way east through Utah.

After eleven months, Carson finally returned to Bent's Fort in July 1844. Within a week, he had set out for Taos and his wife, Josefa. The reunion was short-lived. In August 1845, Carson received a message from Frémont, now a brevet captain, to meet him at Bent's Fort; his guiding services were once again needed for Frémont's third expedition.

Before Carson left to join Frémont, he made arrangements for Josefa to stay with her sister, Ignacia Bent, at her home in Taos. There was an uprising of civil unrest in Taos at the time, and Carson thought his wife would be safe at the Bent home, as Charles Bent was now the governor of Taos. While the Bent family, including Josefa Jaramillo Carson, would experience the ravages of war at their very doorstep, Carson and Frémont, nearly one thousand miles west, would experience the same. Frémont's instructions for this third expedition were to explore the headwaters of the Arkansas and Red Rivers. However, several historians have speculated that Frémont received secret government orders, perhaps from President James Polk, to travel to Mexican California in an effort to gather intelligence and further the government's plan of manifest destiny. As it turns out, this is indeed what occurred.

Frémont's group of nearly one hundred men traversed the rugged Rocky Mountain Range without incident, arriving at Sutter's Fort in December. A few days later, Frémont ventured to Monterey, where he met with both American and Mexican officials. Rebuffed by the Mexican officials, Frémont was ordered to leave the region. Frémont defied the order, and on March 11, 1846, he and his men joined the Bear Flag Revolt, a grassroots organization to free the California region from Mexico. It was a three-year war.

During this time, Carson went from being a guide to an overland dispatcher. Carson carried military dispatches between command posts. When Congress declared war against Mexico on May 13, 1846, Carson's dispatch duties greatly expanded; he was now carrying messages from California to Washington, D.C.

In September 1846, Carson returned to California with news that Mexico had surrendered. With this glorious news, the American flag was raised at every port along the California shoreline. Later, President James K. Polk would declare Carson a hero.

Meanwhile, in Taos, several native Mexicans, as well as many of the local Taos Indians, resented the American takeover of their land. Rioting in the streets of Taos became a revolt full of violence and murder. Before dawn on the cold morning of Friday, January 16, bedlam broke out on the streets of Taos when a group of Taos Indians, led by Tomasito Romero, stormed into the local jail and broke out two of their tribal members, who were being held on petty charges.[13]

By the time Sheriff Stephen Louis Lee arrived at the jail, a large group of angry and quite inebriated men had formed a mob. As the group grew larger by the hour, Sheriff Lee was powerless to stop them. Cornelio Vigil, Governor Bent's brother-in-law and a member of the government, tried to reason with the unruly men. Suddenly, a few of the men grabbed Vigil and began beating him. Then, others brought out weapons, including knives. When the men started stabbing Vigil repeatedly, others began cutting off his body parts—ears, fingers, legs and arms. Terrified, Sheriff Lee attempted to flee the horrific scene but was caught and killed.

Feeling victorious, Romero led the murderous rioters through Taos to the home of Governor Bent, which was located in the heart of the town plaza. The family was still asleep at that early hour. However, the family cook, who was preparing the morning meal in the kitchen, heard the approaching mob and alerted the governor. At approximately seven o'clock, as the sun was rising, Bent, the only man in residence, quickly dressed and went downstairs. Residing in the Bent home with Maria Ignacia and their children, Alfred, Teresina and Estafina, were Rumalda Bent Boggs, Maria's daughter from a previous marriage and the wife of Thomas Boggs, and Josefa Jaramillo Carson.

While the women and children were safely hidden in an adjoining room, the angry mob shouted and pounded on the door of the Bent home. As Bent opened the door, hoping to reason with the men, he was shot several times. Bent fell back inside the doorway, and Maria rushed toward him. A few of the Taos Indians shot arrows inside the house, with one hitting Maria Ignacia. Still, Maria Ignacia managed to get to the door, close it and bolt it.

In the adjoining room, Josefa and Rumalda used iron spoons and pokers to open a hole in the brick wall of the house. Incredibly, the two young women were eventually able to make an opening large enough for them to get through. Rumalda and Josefa then helped Alfred, Teresina and Estafina through the opening. By this time, the women could hear the sounds of the frenzied mob and knew they had broken into the house. Just as Maria Ignacia managed to get through the hole in the wall, the maniacal mob stormed into the room.

Rumalda Luna Bent Boggs, who was holding her mortally wounded stepfather, looked up in fear when the mob entered the room. Rumalda watched in horror as Tomasito Romero jerked Bent from Rumalda's clutches and threw him to the floor. What happened next is best related by Rumalda Luna Bent Boggs: "He [Romero] proceeded to scalp [Bent] with a bowstring while he was still yet alive, cutting as cleanly with the tight cord as it could have been done with a knife."[14] As Romero and his cohorts began mutilating the lifeless body of Charles Bent, Buenaventura Lobato, one of the instigators of the mob violence, rushed into the Bent home. Disgusted by the bloody remains of Governor Charles Bent, Lobato admonished Romero and the others for killing the governor. Lobato then ordered the men to leave the Bent residence. They did so but not before Romero grabbed the scalp of Charles Bent. Horrified by the death of Charles Bent and the intimidation by the murderous mob, the Bent family remained in the home in a state of shock. Sometime in the early morning the following day, a few neighbors managed to sneak to the Bent house under the cloak of darkness to deliver food to the women and children.

Famed mountain man James Beckwourth, a longtime friend of the Bent brothers, had witnessed the murder and rode through the night and for half a day to reach Bent's Fort with the grim news. But word of mouth traveled faster; Bent family member and frontiersman Charles Autobees had already broken the devastating news to the Bent brothers. William and younger his brother George executed a secret retrieval of Charles's body, which was necessary given the violent climate of the area. Charles Bent was secretly buried near a wall at Bent's Fort, next to the grave of his youngest brother, Robert, who was also murdered on October 20, 1841, scalped by Comanche Indians along the Santa Fe Trail. Several years later, the body of Charles Bent was returned to Santa Fe and given an honorable burial.[15] Romero and his violent mob continued their rampage through the streets of Taos and the surrounding area. Perhaps on instructions from Lobato, the rioters seemed to target members of Governor Bent's family and those in political office associated with him. As the marauders moved through the town, they carried a large wooden board with the scalp of Governor Charles Bent pinned to it for all to see.

In a stable at the edge of town, the mob cornered two men, Narciso Beaubien and Pablo Jaramillo, the brother of Maria Ignacia Bent and Josefa Carson. The two men had no chance to defend themselves as the murderous mob lanced them to death. Next, the mob found James W. Leal, an attorney in the governor's office. After the mob tortured the young attorney, they scalped him while he was still alive and left him to die on the streets of Taos. Jose Raphael Sena de Luna Sr., Maria Bent's father, was accosted at his home, and much of his property was destroyed. Romero and his thugs also ransacked the home of Christopher "Kit" and Josefa Carson, which was located near Charles Bent's home.

After two days of murderous rampaging, the violence was finally over. A wounded Maria Ignacia Bent, her three children and Rumalda and Josefa finally felt safe enough to leave their home. The women and children joined several other terrified Taos citizens who were offered sanctuary at the fortified home of Padre Antonio José Martínez.

On February 3, 1847, a company of U.S. volunteer troops, led by Ceran Saint Vrain, arrived in Taos. When news of the troops' arrival reached the bloodthirsty mob, they moved to an old mission church, the San Geronimo de Taos, which their Taos Indian allies had taken over. Within days of their arrival, the U.S. Army volunteers attacked the mission compound with heavy artillery. The attack lasted the entire day, with casualties occurring on both sides. During the battle, one of the leaders of the mob faction, Pablo Chavez, was spotted by the soldiers. Chavez was wearing the bloodstained coat of Governor Charles Bent. Ceran Saint Vrain, a close friend of the now-deceased Charles Bent, was incensed at the outrageous sight and put a bullet in the head of Chavez. With that, the Taos revolt was over.

In late February 1847, Carson led a small group back east. It was a difficult trip for the legendary scout. Water was scarce, and Indian threats were constant. Finally, in early April, the group arrived in Santa Fe, where Carson first learned of the Taos revolt. Although Carson had government dispatches that needed to be delivered to Washington, D.C., he immediately left Santa Fe for Taos.

Carson arrived in Taos on April 9, 1847. He must have been relieved to find Josefa alive and well, although she was considerably shaken by the murderous revolt. When Carson took Josefa back to their home, Josefa's niece eight-year-old Teresina Bent came to live with the Carsons. Years later, Teresina Bent described her aunt Josefa:

[She was] *rather dark in complexion, very dark hair, large bright eyes, very well built, graceful in every way, quite handsome,* [a] *very good wife and the best of mothers.*[16]

During this time, Carson spent ten precious days with his wife, whom he had not seen in twenty long months. Still in the employ of the U.S. government, Carson was duty-bound to proceed with the dispatches to the nation's capital.

Carson rode his horse to Saint Louis, Missouri, where he journeyed eastward via steamship and then traveled by rail to Washington, D.C. Carson was met at the depot by Jessie Benton Frémont, the wife of John C. Frémont. On June 7, 1847, Jessie Frémont hosted a meeting in her father Senator Thomas Hart Benton's home between Carson and President James K. Polk. Later that evening, Polk invited Carson to a private meeting.

President Polk was so impressed with Carson's service to the country that on June 9, 1847, he appointed Carson as second lieutenant of the Regiment of Mounted Riflemen. On June 15, Carson left the capital, bound for the New Mexico Territory and Josefa. Again on horseback, Carson made his way west, eventually reaching the Santa Fe Trail, which he followed into Santa Fe. There, he was met by Josefa and her sister Maria Ignacia. It was a short reunion, as Carson had orders from the president to return to California with government dispatches.

Carson arrived in Monterey in October, where he delivered the dispatches to Governor Richard D. Mason. While in the city, Carson met the young army lieutenant William Tecumseh Sherman.

Finally, by October 1848, Carson was back in Taos, where he intended to stay with Josefa. For income, he hired himself out to William Bent and others who needed his services, but he always returned to Taos. Carson had barely been home thirty days when he received word that Frémont was at Bent's Fort and required his services for another expedition west. This time, Carson refused. Perhaps it was in deference to Josefa, or more likely, he did not like the fact that Frémont insisted on leaving in the middle of the winter season. Despite warnings from experienced trappers—even William Bent—Frémont remained adamant. On November 15, 1848, Frémont's group of thirty-four men, with Old Bill Williams as their guide, left Bent's Fort, headed for the Southern Colorado mountains. However, tragedy struck when the group became stranded by a severe snowstorm high in the La Garita Mountains.

Then on February 12, 1849, Frémont and a small group of his men staggered into Carl Beaubien's mercantile. Carson and Lucien Maxwell were in the store at the time. No one recognized the thin, weak, hollow-eyed leader until he said his name: John C. Frémont.[17]

After organizing a search party to rescue the remainder of Frémont's men, Carson brought his good friend to his home. Frémont remained in the Carson home for three weeks as Carson and Josefa cared for him. By March 1, 1849, Frémont was well enough to resume his exploration and left the Carson home. Carson and Frémont remained friends but never saw each other again.

In 1853, Carson also took on a role to serve his country, serving as the federal Indian agent for Northern New Mexico. With a quarterly salary of nearly $400, it provided a good income for Carson's growing family. Carson worked with the Ute and Jicarilla Apache tribes. He would become a good friend and benefactor of Ute chief Ouray. With the heavy impact of the government's westward policy of manifest destiny, Carson understood the Indians' fight to hold onto their lands, yet he also knew the reality: the government would prevail. Thus, Carson advocated the government's creation of reservations.

When war broke out between the states in April 1861, Carson joined the First New Mexico Volunteer Infantry Regiment. Serving as a Union colonel, Carson was stationed in Albuquerque. In December, Carson sent for Josefa and his children to join him there for Christmas.

In early 1862, Carson received orders to move Companies A and G of the First Cavalry south, approximately sixteen miles from the Rio Grande River, in an effort to stop marauding bands of Mescalero Apaches and Navajos. Before he left on his new assignment, Carson made arrangements to get his family safely back to Taos.

Josefa Carson need not have worried about Sibley's "stragglers," as her husband would encounter the Confederate commander in the Battle of Valverde. The Union army was victorious, as Henry Hopkins Sibley and his troops were forced to retreat. With this successful battle, Major General James H. Carleton assigned Carson the task of apprehending the marauding Navajo bands who were raiding communities in the Southern New Mexico Territory.

In the summer of 1863, Carson dutifully carried out his orders. He enlisted the help of neighboring tribes, principally the Utes, to locate the Navajo camps and break their stronghold of the lands. With this accomplished, Carson and his troops pursed the scattered Navajo people. With their camps and livestock destroyed, facing starvation and long cold winter, the Navajo bands eventually arrived at Fort Canby, where they surrendered. It was a brutal military campaign in which Carson successfully completed his assigned duty.

On November 1, 1863, Carson requested a leave of absence. Whether this was due to the long military campaign, his personal beliefs or the ensuing winter weather will never be known. Nevertheless, General Carleton refused the request and ordered Carson to move his troops to the Navajo stronghold of Canyon de Chelly, northwest of Fort Canby. Upon Carson's arrival, Carleton ordered him to "clean out the Navajos from the canyon." By January 1864, Carson had led his troops to a successful campaign against the Navajo throughout Canyon de Chelly. Carson and his officers arrived in Santa Fe in the last week of January. After meeting with Carleton, Carson was allowed a brief leave of absence and returned to Taos.

The fact was that forty-four-year-old Kit Carson was not in good health. An injury he acquired in 1860 after falling from a horse was beginning to bother him. Carson also tired of the long absences from his family.

Major General James H. Carleton was a difficult man to serve under. Not only did he deny Carson's request for a new assignment, but he also refused to accept Carson's resignation. Instead, on May 30, Carleton ordered Carson to report to Fort Sumner and the Bosque Redondo Reservation, where he would become supervisor of the nearly eight thousand Navajo captives. Carson was appalled at the deplorable health conditions at the reservation. The Indians were malnourished and living in filth. Carson tried to improve the situation but was rebuffed by fort commander Captain Henry B. Bristol. Carson was so enraged that he again submitted his resignation.

(*Seated, left to right*): Colonel D.H. Rucker, Kit Carson, Brevet Brigadier General James H. Carleton. (*Standing left to right*): Colonel E.H. Bergmann, Delegate Charles P. Clever, Colonel Nelson H. Davis, Colonel Herbert M. Enos, Surgeon Basil K. Norris and Colonel J.C. McFerran. Image taken in 1866. *Palace of the Governors Photograph Archives; New Mexico History Museum (Santa Fe, NM); public domain.*

Again, Carleton refused the resignation. Carson was ordered to recruit as many Ute scouts as possible for an upcoming campaign against the Comanche and Kiowa Indian tribes.

On October 22, 1864, Carson led an expedition of three hundred troops of the First Cavalry, New Mexico Volunteers, and seventy Ute scouts and warriors along the Canadian River and into the Texas Panhandle. Carson's group set up camp at Adobe Walls, the abandoned trading post established by the Bent brothers. On the morning of November 25, 1864, Ute scouts discovered the camp of the targeted marauding Comanche and Kiowa bands, estimated to number over one thousand.

Carson ordered troops to bring forth the two howitzers and position one on the north side of the river and the other on the south side. By mid-morning, Carson's troops were in place and attacked the encampment. The battle raged on for six long hours before the Indians, suffering severe casualties, retreated. Before dusk, Carson ordered troops to enter the camp and burn it.

Following the battle of Adobe Walls, Carson remained in military service under Carleton, although he no longer served as field commander. On March 13, 1865, at Carleton's recommendation, Carson received the rank of brevet brigadier general.

Nearly a year later, Carson received another promotion: commander of Fort Garland.

At the end of the Civil War, an even greater westward migration occurred, as federal land grants attracted thousands seeking opportunity. This increase in population often caused hostility among the Native Americans, particularly the Ute bands of the area. As the Ute raids in the San Luis Valley intensified, General John Pope of Fort Union wrote a recommendation to General William Tecumseh Sherman in August 1866, regarding Carson. Because of this, Sherman offered Carson a military appointment.

Carson accepted General Sherman's appointment as commander of Fort Garland on May 19, 1866. He had dealt with the Utes for years, knew their language and had become friends with many, including Ute chief Ouray. General Sherman met with Carson at the fort in September 1866 to discuss treaties with the Utes. "His integrity is simply perfect," Sherman later wrote.

Carson moved his family to the Southern Colorado fort, where they lived in the commandant's quarters while Carson was in command. The fort was in bad condition when Carson arrived, and he had his work cut out for him. Nevertheless, the entire force of ten officers and sixty-three soldiers were there to greet their new commander.

Soldiers at Fort Garland. *Public domain.*

Carson felt that the scant military presence in the region had to be apparent to the local Indians. Carson's approach was to work for peace with the Indian tribes. Nevertheless, he felt the fort was "inadequate for the proper protection of government property alone."

In a rare act of friendship and trust, Ouray brought his band of Utes to Fort Garland, where he and Carson worked together to negotiate peace. Through their work, Carson and Ouray were able to strike peace with the Utes, which lasted for the next decade in the San Luis Valley.

Commander Christopher "Kit" Carson remained in charge of Fort Garland until November 22, 1867, when he was mustered out of service, at his request. During the Christmas season of 1867, Kit Carson; his wife, Maria Josefa Jaramillo Carson; and their six children moved to Boggsville in the southeastern area of Colorado Territory. Thomas O. Boggs immediately offered his in-laws, the Carson family, the adjoining three vacant rooms of a six-room adobe outbuilding. John Carson, a direct descendant of Carson, later remarked:

Back then, you had to work together with people in order to survive. Boggsville gave permanency to the area. People knew they would be treated well there. It was a haven where they wouldn't be cheated.

Josefa must have been happy to be reunited with her sister Maria Ignacia, who lived with the Boggs family, as well as her niece Rumalda Boggs, Thomas's wife.

However, upon Carson's arrival at Boggsville, it was obvious to all that his health was declining. Carson must have realized it as well. Not long after his family had settled into their new home, which Carson hoped was temporary, he traveled a few miles to the home of his old friend William Bent. It was during this visit that Carson met Dr. Henry R. Tilton, the army surgeon at Fort Lyon. After a casual conversation, Carson told the doctor of his ailments.

Dr. Tilton offered to take Carson in his carriage to Fort Lyon for a detailed consultation. After a rigorous exam, Carson was diagnosed with an aneurysm of the carotid artery. Doctor Henry R. Tilton later described the sad event:

The General, as Carson was popularly and officially known, now was a sick man, without long-assured income, [and] *was the sole support of a goodly family, and was facing evil days.*

Josefa, who was present when the doctor gave the couple the devastating news, struggled amid her pregnancy to keep both her husband and children in optimistic spirits. Her niece Rumalda Boggs helped with the children and the cooking and cleaning, which provided time for Josefa to rest and take care of herself and her unborn baby. In late January 1868, General Carson was among the many Colorado dignitaries called to Washington, D.C., by the War Department for a conference on how best to prevent Indian uprisings. Despite his declining health, Carson agreed to accompany Colorado governor Alexander C. Hunt and a Ute delegation of chiefs, including his friend Chief Ouray, for a peace council with President Andrew Johnson.

On the return trip, Carson became very ill, yet managed to make it to his home in Boggsville. Two days later, on April 13, 1868, Carson's wife, Josefa, gave birth to the couple's seventh child. While the baby girl was healthy, Josefa was quite weak and remained in bed for days. Carson sat by his wife's side, confident Josefa would be fine.

Sadly, on April 27, 1868, Josefa died.[18] Kit Carson gave the baby a name, Josefita, in honor of her mother and his beloved wife. Perhaps due to his grief, Carson's poor health rapidly deteriorated. On May 14, 1868, Thomas Boggs hitched his wagon and drove the ailing Carson to Fort Lyon. There, Dr. Henry R. Tilton thoroughly examined Carson. Dr. Tilton later described the situation:

> *His* [Carson's] *disease, aneurysm of the aorta, had progressed rapidly; and the tumor pressing on the pneumo-gastric nerves and trachea caused frequent spasms of the bronchial tubes, which were exceedingly distressing.*

Opposite: Kit Carson died in what is today the Fort Lyon Chapel. *Carol M. Highsmith, 1946; Carol M. Highsmith Archive; Library of Congress.*

Above: Kit Carson was buried next to his wife in Boggsville. Their bodies were later interred at the cemetery in Taos, New Mexico. *Author's collection.*

Fearing Carson would not live much longer, Dr. Tilton moved the Civil War general to the chapel for his comfort as well as his privacy. For the next two weeks, Dr. Tilton tended to his only patient day and night, doing what he could to ease Carson's pain. He encouraged Carson to write out his last will, which the dying man did. Carson named Thomas and Rumalda Boggs the guardians of his children, and he named Boggs the executor of his estate. At 4:25 p.m. on May 23, 1868, Carson began coughing, and blood spurted from his mouth. "I supported his forehead on my hand while death speedily closed the scene," wrote Dr. Tilton. Carson's last words in Spanish were, "Adios compadre."

With the passing of General Carson, the commander of Fort Lyon ordered the American flag that was flying high over Fort Lyon be lowered to half-mast in honor of the general. The following day, after a brief ceremony, which included rifle volleys and the playing of Taps, Fort Lyon soldiers led a procession to Boggsville with the casket of General Carson. Upon their arrival at Boggsville on that solemn day, the soldiers carried the casket to the grave next to that of Carson's beloved wife, Josefa.

A year later, almost to the day, Thomas O. Boggs, the executor of Carson's will, disinterred the bodies of Kit and Josefa Carson and transported them to Taos, New Mexico, for a final burial, according to Carson's wishes. In a private ceremony, the bodies of Mr. and Mrs. Christopher "Kit" Carson were buried in the Taos cemetery near the town plaza. For several decades, Carson's older sons Christopher Carson Jr. and Charles cared for their parents' grave site, although there was no headstone.

In 1908, the Taos Masons placed an engraved marble headstone at Kit Carson's grave. Carson's sons followed with a smaller marble stone for their mother, Josefa. In time, a wrought-iron fence was erected around the Carson family plot, and the couple's youngest child, Josefita Carson Squire, was buried next to the parents she never knew. Today, the cemetery is part of Kit Carson Memorial Park. An American flag flies over the cemetery and the town plaza twenty-four hours a day, commemorating an event during the Civil War when the flag and the town were threatened by Confederate sympathizers. It was Kit Carson who led a band of soldiers to guard the town and the flag day and night. It is fitting that the town of Taos return the favor with a flag flying day and night of the grave of their war hero.

In Colorado, the frontier legacy of General Christopher Houston "Kit" Carson lives on. The town of Kit Carson is obviously named for him, as is the army base Fort Carson.

4

FORT LYON

As one of the oldest existing forts in the state, Fort Lyon has been in constant service for over 150 years. Constructed in 1861, the fort was the center for military campaigns, including the Battle of Glorieta Pass, the only Civil War battle fought in the West. Conversely, it was also the staging point for Colonel John M. Chivington's march to the peaceful Cheyenne village at Sand Creek, which resulted in the murder of nearly 150 innocent Arapaho and Cheyenne.

In 1853, William Bent built a second fort commonly known as Bent's New Fort, located in the Big Timbers of the Santa Fe Trail. The stockade was constructed on elevated ground overlooking the Arkansas River, with a commanding view from all directions. Built of local stone with walls that were ten feet high, the trading post served the local settlers as well as the Indians of the area. Through these high walls, legendary frontiersmen, such as James P. Beckwourth and Christopher "Kit" Carson, as well as Cheyenne chief Black Kettle, entered into trade with William Bent. In the fall of 1860, Major General John Sedgwick of the First Cavalry received orders from Brevet Lieutenant General Winfield Scott, commander of the U.S. War Department, to build a new military post at Big Timbers. After surveying the area, Sedgwick sent a report to the assistant adjutant general suggesting the government buy Bent's New Fort. Sedgwick wrote, in part, "I would strongly urge that it [Bent's Fort] be purchased. It is offered for sale for twelve thousand dollars, and I do not think the government can put up such a work for that money."

New Fort Lyon postcard, circa 1900–10. *Public domain.*

On September 9, 1860, Bent signed a temporary lease with Lieutenant James B. McIntyre, the regimental quartermaster. Within a year, the government had revoked Bent's signed lease of Bent's New Fort. Soldiers assigned to the compound fortified and enlarged the complex. Apparently when Bent left the fort, he took everything with him, as the soldiers soon discovered.

> *Inside of the loose stone corrals, no furniture was seen—nothing but bare walls and dirt floors. Decreasing snow banks marked the deficiencies in the roofs, and there was not a foot of lumber within 200 miles with which to remedy the defects. Nice quarters, were they not? We stole and cut up wagon boxes for bunks and tables, bought a set of dishes and some cooking utensils and lived to suit ourselves while we remained there.*[19]

Modifications to the fort included two cavalry stables and two buildings for company quarters. A new stone guardhouse was constructed, along with two buildings for the officers' quarters. Also completed was a twenty-six-bed hospital. There was a great need, as twenty-four of the three hundred soldiers had contracted scurvy due to the lack of fresh fruits and vegetables. By late October, much of the new fort was complete. James H. Haynes, an independent contractor in the Arkansas Valley, sent a progress report to William N. Byers, the owner and publisher of the *Rocky Mountain News*. Byers printed the report in the October 31, 1860 issue, which read, in part:

There are five stables measuring 250 x 150 feet, with stone walls 9 feet high and 2 feet thick, and six barracks, as well as a hospital, guardhouse and bakehouse. 165 six-mule loads of stone were quarried, hauled, and placed. In a little more than six weeks, 128,000 cubic feet of stone were placed in construction.

When completed, the newly refurbished and expanded military fort was named Fort Wise in honor of Henry Alexander Wise, the governor of Virginia. The name was changed when that state seceded from the Union in 1861. During the fort's six years of existence, several historic events occurred there.

A.B. Greenwood, the commissioner of Indian affairs, was eager to negotiate a new peace treaty with the Arapaho and Cheyenne. There was also an ulterior reason for a new treaty: land. The previous year, large amounts of gold had been discovered in the Rocky Mountains. Thousands of gold seekers were rushing to the mountains via the Santa Fe Trail. Albert Gallatin Boone, the grandson of famed frontiersman Daniel Boone, had replaced William Bent as Indian agent in 1860. Through a joint effort between Boone and Bent, they were able to bring several bands of the Arapaho and Cheyenne together for a peace council at Fort Wise.

Commissioner Greenwood and his entourage, followed by thirteen wagons loaded with with goods and presents, arrived at Fort Wise on February 18, 1861. Among the Indians camped near the fort were Left Hand and Little Raven's band of Arapaho. A few days later, Cheyenne leaders Black Kettle, White Antelope, Lean Bear and Tall Bear arrived with their bands, along with Satank and his Kiowa band. Robert Bent, the son of William Bent and Owl Woman, served as the official interpreter for the U.S. government.

The new treaty offered the tribes nearly $500,000 over a fifteen-year period. In return, the treaty required that the Arapaho and Cheyenne relinquish the vast majority of their land appropriated in the Fort Laramie Treaty of 1851. This new proposal reduced their land to one small portion on the Arkansas River in Southern Colorado Territory. However, it also provided each Indian forty acres of land.

The agreement was signed by all in attendance on February 18, 1861. Indian Agent Boone returned to Washington, D.C., with the signed document, which was subsequently ratified in the U.S. Senate and signed by President Abraham Lincoln on December 15, 1861. It was a fabulous treaty for the government. It had acquired the desired land, where gold had recently been discovered, and confined the Indians to a small piece of land far away from the anticipated economic boom. Meanwhile, the Civil War continued in the East. On August 10, 1861, Union general Nathaniel Lyon was killed in the Battle of Wilson's Creek, near Springfield, Missouri. Lyon was the first Union general to be killed in battle. In honor of his service, the fort was renamed Fort Lyon.

In February 1862, Colonel John M. Chivington led the First Regiment of Colorado Volunteers from Camp Weld near Denver to Fort Lyon. Rumors of Confederates invading the Rocky Mountain region for the gold had been swirling ever since the war broke out the previous year. Confederate brigadier general Henry Hopkins Sibley had plans known as the New Mexico Campaign to invade the region near Colorado's border with New Mexico Territory and then move on to the California gold fields. After a few days at Fort Lyon, Chivington and his five hundred soldiers left for Fort Union. On March 26, 1862, Sibley's Brigade, three hundred strong, was on a scouting expedition at Glorieta Pass at the southern tip of the Sangre de Cristo Mountains. It was also a strategic location along the Santa Fe Trail. Sibley's Brigade was met by Union forces led by Colonel John P. Slough and Colonel Chivington. In the two-day battle, Chivington led a bold circular maneuver, taking his men to the rear of Sibley's line. After destroying the Confederate supply lines, Sibley's men were forced to retreat. The Battle of Glorieta Pass, the only Civil War battle in the West, became known as the "Gettysburg of the West," which effectively ended the Confederate presence in the West. Chivington and his men returned to Denver as heroes.

In November 1864, Fort Lyon was the staging point for possibly the worst stain in Colorado's history. Colonel John Chivington led his volunteer soldiers through an all-night snowstorm to Fort Lyon. There, he forced the soldiers into a lockdown situation. No one was allowed in or out. Irving Howbert, who served under Chivington, later recalled the incident: "We arrived at Fort Lyons [sic] about four o'clock in the afternoon of November 28, to the great surprise of its garrison, as they were not aware that the regiment had left the vicinity of Denver. A picket was thrown around the fort at once to prevent the trappers or Indian traders, who generally hung around such places, from notifying the savages of our presence."[20]

Meeting with Major Scott Anthony, the commander of Fort Lyon, Chivington revealed his plan to attack the Indians. Anthony agreed with Chivington's mission but requested that three white men who camped with the Indians, Watson Clark, Private David Louderback and John Smith, be removed from the camp before the attack. He also asked that the peaceful Indian chiefs, Black Kettle, Left Hand, One-Eye and White Antelope, be spared.

At eight o'clock that night, Chivington led the soldiers from Fort Lyon fourteen miles to the banks of Sand Creek. Included in the group were over seven hundred troops comprising the First Colorado Cavalry, as well as the Colorado Third Infantry under Colonel George L. Shoup and additional troops from Fort Lyon under Major Anthony.

At dawn on the morning of November 29, 1864, Chivington ordered his men to fire on the peaceful Indian camp at Sand Creek. When the killing stopped, some six hours later, an estimated 150 Arapaho and Cheyenne were dead.[21]

Several military inquiries would be held, including one at Fort Lyon. However, because Chivington had resigned his commission, no one was ever held accountable for the atrocity at Sand Creek. In the spring of 1867, heavy flooding of the Arkansas River inundated Fort Lyon. Soldiers relocated the military fort twenty miles upstream on a hill near the mouth of the Purgatoire River. The new vantage point provided protection for the settlers and travelers on the Santa Fe Trail. Large stone buildings were constructed to hold the officers' quarters, barracks, a meeting hall, a mess hall, a blacksmith shop, a hospital, a chapel and cavalry stables. These buildings surrounded a large parade ground in the center of the complex. The grounds surrounding the military base were landscaped in a park-like style. Trees were planted along the roadways, and graveled walkways were laid out throughout the complex. The entrance was graced with tall natural stone posts and an impressive iron gate. The new Fort Lyon opened on June 9, 1867.

At some point during the construction, a detachment of soldiers was sent to the site of old Fort Lyon. The soldiers spent two weeks in the rain and mud, removing the bodies of the dead soldiers buried in the fort's cemetery near Graveyard Creek. The bodies were hauled by wagon to a new cemetery located on the northern edge of the new military post.

In the fall of 1867, the abandoned ruins of old Fort Lyon caught fire. As it happened, Captain George Armes and his troops were passing near the area at the time. In his report, Armes wrote:

> We found the old fort or buildings on fire and plenty of fresh signs of Indians all around us. We arrived just in time to put the fire out. The post having been abandoned, the Indians concluded to burn the buildings, but our arrival was just in time to save the fort.[22]

Shortly after the start of 1868, famed frontiersman General Christopher "Kit" Carson arrived at Fort Lyon from his home in nearby Boggsville. Carson had been ill for some time and sought the advice of several doctors. The army post surgeon, Dr. Henry R. Tilton, agreed to meet with Carson. Following a thorough examination, Dr. Tilton's diagnosis was that Carson suffered from aneurysm of the carotid artery.

Following the death of Carson's wife, Josefa, in April 1868, Carson's health rapidly deteriorated. On May 14, 1868, Thomas Boggs brought the ill Carson to Fort Lyon. Dr. Tilton later said "the tumor pressing on the pneumo-gastric nerves and trachea caused frequent spasms of the bronchial tubes, which were exceedingly distressing."

Knowing Carson would not live much longer, Dr. Tilton moved the Civil War general to the chapel for his comfort and privacy. Late in the afternoon on May 23, 1868, fifty-seven-year-old General Christopher "Kit" Carson died. Almost immediately, the American flag flying high over Fort Lyon was lowered to half-mast in honor of the general. The next day, a military ceremony was held at the parade grounds, which included rifle volleys and the playing of Taps.

Fort Lyon ceased to operate as a military post in 1887, following the end of Indian conflicts. In 1907, the fort was utilized as a tuberculosis treatment center. In 1922, the Veterans Administration maintained the former military compound as a medical center for veterans.

In 1973, the cemetery at Fort Lyon was transferred to the National Cemetery System. As such, in 1950, the Fort Lyon National Cemetery became Colorado's second nationally designated cemetery, following Fort Logan. The cemetery's memorial flag, located in the center of the cemetery, is flanked by bronze plaques commemorating the interred soldiers and

Fort Lyon. *Photograph by Jeffery Beall; Creative Commons Attribution 3.0 Unported.*

Fort Lyon gates. *David W. Haas; Library of Congress.*

their dedication to our country. During 2002, the twelve original buildings remaining on the expanded government complex underwent extensive restoration. Included in this group of buildings was the small two-room stone chapel where Christopher "Kit" Carson died. Its original stained-glass windows were refurbished, and its interior received much-needed attention after years of neglect. Today, the building is known as the Kit Carson Memorial Chapel.

Fort Lyon is now a National Historic Site. Visitors are offered limited access to the site, which includes the historic district, the chapel and the cemetery. The national cemetery is located just inside the iron entrance gate of Fort Lyon. On a bronze plaque near the entrance, the following words are inscribed:

On Fame's eternal camping-ground
Their silent tents are spread,
And Glory guards, with solemn round,
The bivouac of the dead.

5

MOUNTAIN MAN EXTRAORDINAIRE MARIANO MEDINA

T ucked deep in the many crevices of the Rocky Mountain Range, hidden from the white man for centuries, lies a narrow gorge cut through the solid rock by what is known today as the Big Thompson River. The Native American tribes, primarily the Utes, knew the river well. The headwaters of the river begin high in Forest Canyon, at the northern edge of today's Rocky Mountain National Park. The steep terrain and sparse vegetation along the walls of the canyon allow for the free-flowing rush of water downstream, creating rock cliffs that rise several hundred feet into the Rocky Mountain sky. For two miles, the water flows down the canyon, where it gently meanders through a lovely mountain meadow. Later called Cedar Cove, the meadow was a natural warm valley, protected by the canyon above and the surrounding Rocky Mountains. Ute Indians, such as Tabernash and Colorow, brought their tribes to winter in the area, where the protected land held an abundance of game for hunting, as well as fine fishing.

With westward expansion encouraged by the government, scouts, mountain men, trappers and traders followed the river, eventually making their way into the spectacular valley. Most moved on; however, one who stayed was Mariano Medina.

When Mariano Medina finally made Colorado his home in 1858, he was a well-respected member of the famed mountain men of the Rocky Mountains.

Born in Taos, Mexico, on February 20, 1812, Mariano Medina was the son of a French trapper and his Jicarilla Apache wife. When Medina came of age, he worked with his father and learned to trap beaver. Years later,

Mariano Medina
was Loveland's
first settler. *Denver
Public Library*.

Medina struck out on his own, traveling the West and setting trap lines in the region's many rivers. Along the way, he became associated with other mountain men and frontiersmen, such as Jim Bridger, the Bent brothers, Christopher "Kit" Carson and Tom Tobin.

Mariano Medina's favorable reputation grew following a scouting expedition in which his vast knowledge of the wilderness led to the capture of two renegade Ute Indians. Famed explorer John C. Frémont employed Medina in one of his many explorations of the West. In 1844, Medina spent the trapping season in the Snake River country of Eastern Utah. There, he met a French trapper, Louis Elbert Papin, and his Flathead Indian wife, Tacaney. Through several discussions, Medina learned that Papin intended to return to civilization permanently. The dilemma of leaving his pregnant Indian wife behind was solved when Medina agreed to take Tacaney as his wife in return for a few horses. Thus, Tacaney moved into Medina's lodge, and Papin left for parts unknown. When the baby was born, he was named Louis Papin after his biological father. However, when the boy grew older, he changed his surname to Papa.[23]

By the 1840s, the beavers were dying out, and the fur trade was coming to an end. For the next decade, Medina provided a guide service for hunters and adventurers. Medina's stepson, Louis Papin "Papa," recalled his trips with his stepfather to various forts, such as Fort Bridger, Fort Laramie, Fort Vasquez and Bent's Fort.

In the summer of 1858, Medina joined prospectors George Andrew Jackson, Nicholas Janis and Jose de Mirabal at a small settlement along the Big Thompson River. The *Rocky Mountain News* of September 5, 1858, reported:

> *Mr. Ceran Saint Vrain has been seen in the company of Mariano Medina near Estes Park, a family outing with several other famous people— William Gilpin José de Mirabal and William Bent.*

By the spring of 1859, the prospectors had moved on, but Medina stayed. He started his own business, providing rafts to ferry teams across the river, and he charged a hefty price of five dollars in gold for the service. After a prosperous season, Medina spent the next few months constructing a toll bridge. When he completed the bridge, with strong pilings driven into the river bottom on either side, it was sturdy and high enough to withstand the area's high spring runoff and floods. Medina charged one dollar, again in gold, to cross the bridge. In time, travelers dubbed the bridge "Mariano's Crossing." With the success of his enterprise, Medina began constructing a trading post on the north side of the river. The new complex soon became a favorite stopover for the growing numbers of travelers during the western migration period. It was the crossing for several trails. The Texas and Overland Trails crossed here, as did the Denver/Laramie Trail. Offshoots of the Platte River Trail and the Oregon Trail also passed through Medina's land. Several of Medina's mountaineer friends often visited the post. The June 4, 1859 issue of the *Rocky Mountain News* reported:

> *Kit Carson spent the past week with friend Jesus Garcia Mariano Medina at his post in the Big Thompson Canyon.*

Considered the first permanent white resident in the Big Thompson Valley, Medina set out to establish a settlement in the valley. The following year, Medina recruited several families from his hometown of Taos to build that settlement. Medina chose a spot near the site of present-day Loveland as the site of his settlement.

One of the friends Medina recruited was Timothy Goodale and his wife, Jennie. The couple arrived in March 1861. Gooddale noted in his journal that some Arapaho Indians were living a mile or so from Mariano's Crossing on the south side of the Big Thompson River.[24] According to Goodale, the leader of the group was either Niwot or Left Hand.

North of Mariano's Crossing was a band of the Cheyenne led by Big Mouth. Many of the Cheyenne warriors were sent to observe the activity of Medina's operation, particularly his vast horse herd pastured near the Cache la Poudre River. The Cheyenne considered the number of ponies he possessed a warriors' wealth.

On April 17, 1861, a band of Cheyenne Indians drove off sixty of Medina's horses. Medina and his men, including Goodale and Mirabal, tracked the thieves for twenty-five miles. Medina managed to shoot one of the Indians with his Hawken rifle, but the others got away. Three days later, Mariano and his group returned with fifty of the stolen horses, while the Indians had shot five and had gotten away with five.

Following the Indian raid, Medina built a small fort on the north side of the river. Constructed of stone, the fifteen-by-twenty-five-foot structure included two gun ports on three sides. Its walls were eighteen inches thick, and the flat roof made of hand-hewn logs was covered with sandstone slabs topped with a foot of dirt.[25] The following year, Ben Holladay moved his overland stage route from Wyoming to Colorado. Because the new route passed near Mariano's Crossing, Medina's operation expanded to include a stage stop.

In 1868, a post office was established, and Medina's settlement was called Namaqua. Log commercial buildings and residential homes were built. As there was no longer a threat of Indian attacks, Medina's fort was utilized as an icehouse. In his later years, Medina was known as a charitable man, and his charity parties were the talk of the settlement. Medina served his guests fine wines and Santa Fe cuisine he prepared and provided musical entertainment. On other occasions, Medina would show off his famous Hawken muzzle loader that he fondly named "Old Lady Hawkens." Medina would also parade around in his white Spanish-style leather jacket, leather breeches, fancy knitted long socks and beaded moccasins. It is said that the women were charmed by the character of the Spanish gentleman, and the men were impressed with his guns and stories of his early frontier days.

Medina's stepson, Louis Papin Papa, so enjoyed his childhood in the valley of the Big Thompson that he filed for a homestead at Cedar Cove, where he built a fine log cabin. There, he met a newcomer to the area, Frank Bartholf. The two became lifelong friends. Bartolf had homesteaded land a few miles north of Cedar Cove along the Big Thompson River, at a point

Left: The grave of Mariano Medina. *Photograph by Sharon Perry.*

Right: A life-size sculpture sits in the town of Loveland. *Photograph by Sharon Perry.*

where the river forks north toward the Mummy Range (now a portion of the Rocky Mountain National Park). Here, Bartolf built a respectable cattle ranch, which Louis Papin Papa eventually managed. Louis later worked on several cattle ranches in the Estes Park area.

Mariano Medina died on June 28, 1878. Today, Fort Namaqua Park, located nearly halfway between Loveland and Drake at County Road 19E and the Big Thompson River, the site of the trading post and stage station, is one of the earliest historic sites in Colorado. Located here are the grave sites of Medina, his Indian wife and several family members. An impressive stone marker with a plaque marks the site.

> *His post was a known location for the "pony trade," "Whites," "Mexicans" and "Indians" traded on a regular schedule here in the Big Thompson Valley.*

Following in his stepfather's death, Louis Papin Papa was well known and respected in the Loveland area—so much so that he was elected town marshal in 1900. In his later years, he was often seen riding his white horse and wearing his father's fancy clothes, including the famed white breeches and long knitted socks, at various occasions. He was known to ride his horse to a ridge northwest of Loveland, where an Indian burial contained the remains of his family members, including those of his stepsister, Lena. Louis Papin Papa died in 1935.

Today, Fort Namaqua Park stands as a lasting memorial to Mariano Medina, the first settler in the valley of the Big Thompson River.

6

LEGENDARY TRACKER
THOMAS TATE TOBIN

He could track a grasshopper through the sagebrush.

This was one of the many attributes paid to Tom Tobin by his friends on the Colorado frontier. Indeed, Tobin was truly a force to be reckoned with. A scout with excellent tracking skills, Tobin worked with the likes of army colonels Sterling Price and Samuel Tappan in not only forging the frontier of the Colorado Territory but also in several famous incidents of Colorado's early history. It was his exploration, knowledge and keen insight of the land that helped bring settlement to the frontier.

With these skills and the work with the military, Tobin's reputation, while well known among the frontiersmen in Southeastern Colorado, grew considerably across Colorado Territory. Tobin kept company with the likes of Christopher "Kit" Carson, Jim Bridger, James Beckwourth, the Bent brothers and Ceran Saint Vrain. Thomas Tate Tobin is considered one of the most adventurous frontiersmen who blazed the trail for permanent settlement.

Thomas Tate Tobin was born in Saint Louis, Missouri, on May 1, 1823. His father, Bartholomew Tobin, was an Irish immigrant who had married a young widow, Sarah Tate Autobees, in Saint Louis the previous year. Sarah, a light-skinned "mulatto" woman from Nova Scotia, had married François Autobees in 1811. The following year, a son, Charles, was born. Three years later, Autobees drowned while on a river expedition in Canada. Bartholomew Tobin and Sarah Tate Autobees were married in 1821. In 1823, she gave birth to Thomas Tate Tobin. A year later, a daughter, Catherine, was born.

Famed scoutsman Tom Tobin tracked down the bloody Espinosa brothers. *History Colorado; public domain.*

Thomas Tate Tobin was to lead an adventurer's lifestyle. At five feet, seven inches tall—considered average for the time—his swarthy complexion and facial features always puzzled those who attempted to guess his nationality. Known for his short temper, ready to fight at the drop of a hat, Tobin was a deadly shot with either a rifle or pistol, but not a kinder man could be found when he was talking to friends—"A person never left his camp hungry or penniless, a man of his word."

In 1828, at the age of sixteen, Charles Autobees left home to join the beaver trappers who were heading west. He returned to Saint Louis in 1837 to fetch his half brother, fourteen-year-old Tom. Tobin spent the next few years working with his half brother, Charles. The two delivered dry food supplies, "Taos Lightning" and whiskey to frontier outposts; they also traded for beaver pelts and buffalo skins. Included in their itinerary was Fort Jackson (which later became Fort Lupton), Bent's Fort and El Pueblo. The newly acquired pelts and skins were either traded at other forts or taken to Saint Louis annually by William Bent.

For the next several years, Tobin worked for the Bent brothers at their fort on the Arkansas River. It was here that he became an expert trapper and scout, and he honed his tracking skills. Tobin was famous for his uncanny ability to detect and follow signs. It was Tobin's keen skills that led to him gaining a reputation as a great frontiersman, which would serve him well throughout his life time.

Dr. Edgar L. Hewett, an archaeologist, knew Tobin well and even hunted with him in the 1890s. Dr. Hewett later wrote of his friend:

> Tobin gained his great reputation as a trail man by his uncanny ability to detect and follow "sign." He could track a grasshopper through sagebrush. Those who had seen him on the trail told me that he always took the most likely starting point, swung round and round in ever-widening circles until he cut sign then clung to his sign until his quarry was overtaken. It was a technique he had learned from the Indians, with whom he had often fought and, in better times, traded. When tracking, he often got down on all fours with his face close to the ground, following sign that was imperceptible to less-acute eyes.[26]

In 1844, Tobin was living south of the U.S. border, where he quickly learned the Spanish language and became a naturalized citizen. At the age of twenty-one, Tobin joined the Roman Catholic Church in order to marry fifteen-year-old Maria Pascuala Bernal. In what would turn out to be a strange twist of fate, Maria was the daughter of Felipe Espinosa y Bernal and Maria Candelaria de Herrera. Therefore, through her father, Maria was related to Felipe Espinosa, whom Tobin would later kill. Padre José Martínez, who officiated Tobin's wedding ceremony, was also believed to be the "superior" of the local religious hierarchy. Thus, ironically enough, Padre Martínez may also have been a mentor to the notorious Espinosa brothers, Felipe and Vivian.[27]

By 1846, following the war between Mexico and the United States, Tobin and his wife, Maria, were living at Arroyo Hondo on a ranch Tobin had built. This ranch was located a few miles north of Taos, New Mexico, a place Charles Bent had first brought Tobin to.

Civil unrest remained following the war, particularly in the Taos area. It was at his ranch that Tobin received military orders through General Stephen Kearny to carry secret dispatches to military authorities at Fort Leavenworth. Traveling alone and with no word to anyone, save the military, Tobin carried out his duties undetected. At times, he would acquire a fresh horse from the Indians without their knowledge.

Eventually returning to his home and family, Tobin found himself involved in a rebellion that would end in murder—the death of his beloved friend, Charles Bent.

Several Mexican nationalists from Santa Fe, under the direction of Pablo Montoya and Thomas Romero, attacked Turley's mill and distillery. Tobin and another American, Johnnie Albert, were the only ones who escaped with their lives from the burning building. Following this incident, Tobin and his half brother, Charles Autobees, were the first to join a detachment led by Captain Ceran Saint Vrain to find the insurrectionists.

For over a month, the same group of Santa Fe men planned a massive attack on the citizens of Taos. Boiling feelings of revenge and hatred spilled over into the streets of Taos on the night of January 19, 1847. The group broke into the home of New Mexico governor Charles Bent. They killed and then scalped Governor Bent, the sheriff and several men in the immediate area, while the women and children fled. Among them were the wives and children of Kit Carson and Thomas Boggs. Tobin, who was in the area, ran to the aid of his friend Charles Bent but to no avail. With buildings burning and fires set in alleyways, Tobin managed to escape the carnage. The following day, an Indian runner came into Taos with a notice from the conspirators promising revenge against the Americans and murder to their enemy: the Catholic Church. Military troops from Santa Fe soon arrived, led by General Stephen Kearny and Captain Ceran Saint

Captain Ceran Saint Vrain.
History Colorado; public domain.

Vrain, who immediately recruited Tobin and his half brother, Charles Autobees, to join their detachment in tracking down the insurrectionists. Another legendary scout, James Beckwourth, joined the military group. Within a few short days, the three scouts were following the trail of the outlaws and were successful in surrounding the group. A short battle of resistance ensued, and a few of the conspiring group were killed. Tobin and his men brought the others to Santa Fe, where they were later tried, convicted and hanged.

Two years later, almost to the day of the Taos uprising, Tobin received a message from his old friend Christopher "Kit" Carson. Army major general B.L. Beall was planning a military expedition along the Arkansas River and had asked Carson to lead the scouting team. Carson recruited both Tobin and his half brother, Charles Autobees. The military mission, on information provided by Indian Agent Thomas Fitzpatrick, was to locate and rescue a group of Mexicans who were being held by a band of the Kiowa. Tobin was later described by Major General Beall as "having a reputation almost equal to Kit Carson's for bravery, dexterity with his rifle, and skill in mountain life."

By 1852, Tobin had moved his family north into what would become Colorado Territory. Tobin and Autobees offered their services in the building of Fort Massachusetts. The first U.S. military post established in the northernmost area of the Department of New Mexico, the fort, located in a sheltered valley on Ute Creek, was located approximately eighty miles north of Taos. When the fort opened on June 22, 1852, Tobin served as a scout for its troops.

In 1858, Brigadier General John Garland had received orders to construct a new fort to replace the insufficient Fort Massachusetts. The new fort, located six miles north, was named Fort Garland after the general. The construction of the fort, under the direction of Tobin's half brother, the veteran frontiersman Charles Autobees, was built of adobe brick. A few days into the construction, a local worker by the name of Juan Pineda stabbed Autobees through his left arm and into his breast, the blade coming close to his heart. With Autobees in such a perilous, life-threatening condition, Tobin

The front gate of Fort Garland. *Public domain.*

took over the construction for his injured brother.[28] When the construction was completed, the location of the new fort provided an unobstructed view from every direction, making it an excellent defensive position.

Later, Tobin returned to his small ranch, which was located along the San Carlos River southeast of El Pueblo, where he spent his time farming and raising his five children.[29] Tobin sold his produce to a military squad led by Lieutenant Colonel William Gilpin. The troops were camped near Bent's Fort. During this time, Tobin and Gilpin, who would later become the first territorial governor of Colorado, became good friends. All the while, Tobin's scouting and tracking abilities remained in high demand. The following year, Gilpin recruited Tobin to scout for him during a campaign against the Indians. Tobin also served as a courier, carrying dispatches from the Canadian River Valley of Oklahoma to Bent's Fort. Shortly after this expedition, Tobin retired from scouting and returned to his ranch and family.

The summer of 1863 was the last season that forty-year-old Tobin traded with the Arapaho and Cheyenne at Bent's Fort and Fort Garland. In the fall of 1863, Tom Tobin was called out of retirement. In the spring of 1863, the settlers and townsfolk from Colorado City to Florissant were terrorized by a couple of thugs who took on a crazed notion of revenge and retribution against all white settlers. Fear spread throughout the area, as random killings continued with no knowledge of the killers. With no telegraph lines, news traveled slowly, which added to the fear in the surrounding area.

All the killings were the same. The naked corpses were left sprawled out on the muddy blood-soaked ground; the victims had been hacked to death, their skulls cracked open. For those who discovered the remains, they were horrific sights. Then the shocking news came that another murder had occurred in the area now known as Dead Man's Canyon, and this murder was the same as the others. What struck the community to the core was that this victim was one of their own. William Bruce was well respected in the community, running a sawmill not far from the first killings. His wife had reported him missing on Monday, March 16, 1863, after he did not return from a business meeting. His body, found in the canyon, was shot full of bullets. Powder burns on his body suggested close-range fire, and his chest had been hacked with an axe. Two days later, on Wednesday, March 18, a third murder in the canyon occurred. The naked and mutilated body of Henry Hawkins, an elderly, reclusive man, was found on the banks of Little Fountain Creek, near Dead Man's Canyon.[30] Within two days, the lawmen of the area knew who they were after. But tracking them was another matter.

The Espinosa Gang from New Mexico was a small group of brothers and cousins led by Felipe Nerio Espinosa and his brother Vivian Espinosa. Local law enforcement theorized that the murderous gang had moved north with these recent killings and were now exacting their revenge on settlers of Colorado Territory. Meanwhile, as the authorities were trailing these murderous outlaws, another murder rocked the Florissant area. The mail carrier came into Florissant at a breakneck speed and in a horrific panic. He reported that the body of John Addleman, a member of the Florissant community, had been found lying near the house at his ranch west of the Platte River, just a few miles from the modern town of Florissant. John Addleman was the son of a supreme court justice from Pennsylvania, and he was well respected in the area.

While the community prepared for his funeral, the lawmen hit the outlaws' new trail from Canyon City, north to the South Park region and to California Gulch in Lake County. While the posse was in pursuit of the murderers, Vivian Espinosa was killed.

The murderers were now thought to be retreating south via Ute Pass country, back to the New Mexico Territory. As the news came into Florissant and authorities continued to pursue the case, fear gripped the area. It was learned that Espinosa's nephew sixteen-year-old José Vincente Espinosa had replaced the murdered Vivian, and the gang's vendetta continued, as six more victims fell before their guns. People kept close to home and seldom came to town. Those in town kept a watchful eye out for strangers or unusual conditions.

Unknown to anyone at the time was the fact that, at some point soon after the death of Vivian Espinosa, his brother Felipe Nerio Espinosa returned to the site in the canyon to recover his skeletal remains.[31] In an incredibly bizarre act, Felipe cut off the foot of his brother before reburying the body. Years later, when Felipe's sister-in-law, Eugenia H. Lucero, died at the age of 106, her obituary included information regarding Vivian Espinosa's severed foot.

The Espinosa brothers' trail from Florissant went into the South Park area and Park County. Local law enforcement, now handled by Park County officials, worked continuously on the case, learning many facts, but the desperadoes remained elusive.

In October 1863, the murderous Espinosa Gang struck again. Leander Philbrook and Delores Sanchez were traveling in a buckboard from Trinidad to Fort Garland. Suddenly, while they were traversing the Sangre de Cristo Canyon, shots rang out, echoing off the canyon walls. Philbrook whipped his mules into a run, but two more shots rang out. Two of the mules dropped dead. Felipe Espinosa and his nephew José came out from behind the rock where they had fired the shots and, with their guns drawn, confronted the couple. Both Philbrook and Sanchez managed to get away. When Philbrook ran up the side of the mountain, the Espinosas chased him. This allowed Sanchez to run in the opposite direction and eventually find a hiding place behind a boulder. It was at this moment that another buckboard, driven by two Hispanic men, arrived at the scene. Dolores Sanchez bolted from her hiding place and ran to the men. In a frantic state, Sanchez explained to the driver, Pedro Garcia, what had just transpired. Garcia helped her into the buckboard and hid her under their provisions as best as possible. Felipe and his nephew José saw the second buckboard and came down the mountain to investigate. The two outlaws interrogated the men, asking if they had seen anyone in the area, to which Garcia answered in the negative. Not convinced, Felipe Espinosa began to rummage through the buckboard. Not wanting to jeopardize the life of Garcia, Sanchez raised her head above the cover. Felipe demanded Sanchez to get out of the buckboard. Sanchez did so and pleaded for Garcia's life to be spared. As José began tying Sanchez's hands and feet, Felipe helped himself to sacks of flour, bread and beans from Garcia's buckboard. Then Garcia was allowed to leave the scene.

After having their way with helpless woman, the two left the bound Sanchez and resumed their hunt for Philbrook. However, unknown to the Espinosas, Philbrook had managed to get out of the canyon and make his way to Fort Garland. As soon as the Espinosas had left in pursuit of Philbrook, Sanchez was able to free herself and flee the area, finally finding a large boulder to hide behind for the night.

Meanwhile, Philbrook walked into Fort Garland at approximately eleven o'clock at night. The twelve-mile walk had caused his feet to bleed from blisters. Philbrook was brought to Colonel Samuel Tappan, who heard his story of capture and escape from the bloody Espinosa Gang. Tappan ordered a detachment of troops to leave at sunrise to rescue Delores Sanchez. However, at daybreak the following morning, Sanchez had left her hiding spot and begun her own long walk to Fort Garland. After approximately two miles, she happened upon two Mexicans who were traveling on horseback. Briefly explaining her plight, she offered four dollars to the men if they would take her to Fort Garland. The men refused, believing Felipe Espinosa would kill them if he found out.[32] After a few more miles, Delores Sanchez finally met the army troops who had come to her rescue. By noon, the troops had arrived back at the fort and arranged medical attention for Delores Sanchez.

Perhaps out of desperation, Territorial Governor John Evans ordered Colonel Sam Tappan, the commander of Fort Garland, to request Tom Tobin's services in the apprehension of the Espinosa Gang. Governor Evans's order was somewhat controversial, as it was issued directly to Tappan rather than Tappan's superior officer, Colonel John M. Chivington.

On October 11, 1863, when Thomas Tate Tobin walked into Fort Garland, he was the quintessential frontiersman. Tobin was dressed in a fringed buckskin coat, complete with a bead-worked waistcoat, bear fur hat and deerskin moccasins. Around his waistcoat were handmade holsters created from the rump of a buffalo. The holsters held Tobin's prized 1851 Colt revolvers. Tobin also carried his .53-caliber Hawken rifle. The firearm,

Soldiers at Fort Garland. *Public domain.*

which was four feet long and weighed sixteen pounds, had ten notches in its barrel, representing the ten men Tobin had killed.[33]

Tobin was offered a reward of $2,500 to track down the murderous gang. While Tobin refused military protection, he did request the assistance of fourteen-year-old Juan Montoya, who was in the employ of Captain W.A. Van Vliet.

On the morning of Monday, October 12, 1863, Tom Tobin left Fort Garland with the teenaged Montoya and Loren Jenks, who occasionally worked as a scout at the fort. Lieutenant H.W. Baldwin also left the fort that morning with a detachment of fifteen soldiers. Tappan's orders were for Baldwin to follow any sign of the Espinosas and report if there was a possibility of their capture. Believing it would be a long search, Baldwin's detachment left with six days' rations. They were not needed.

By midafternoon on that first day, Tobin and his small party had found the trail of the bloody Espinosas. Tobin later said:

> Me and four soldiers chased them through heavy pine and quaking aspen, but they got away from us. I then went and took their pony tracks and followed to a branch that was full of pebbles. They took up this branch. I told Lieut. Baldwin to go down this branch till he came to the valley and then stop till I came to him. The Mexican boy discovered the two assassins and told Lieut. Baldwin, "There goes two men on horseback," but he could not make the Lieut. understand until he showed him the pony track. They were then just going out of sight over the ridge, were out of sight too quick for the soldiers to shoot. We then struck down the canyon towards Fort Garland and camped that night.[34]

The following morning, Tobin resumed his search. Finding tracks of Ute Indian ponies, Tobin moved on, but Baldwin and his soldiers did not. Shortly after sunrise on Thursday, October 13, 1863, the third day of tracking the desperados, Tobin and his men resumed their search. By midmorning, Tobin had found recent tracks of two oxen. Finally, Tobin and his group were closing in on their prey.

The site of the Espinosa camp has been described as being near the headwaters of the Quindaro Creek, very near the summit of Veta Mountain in the Sangre de Cristo Mountain Range. Tobin's moccasins made no sound as he advanced toward the campsite very cautiously and slowly. When he spotted the Espinosas at the campsite, Tobin stopped. The veteran scout prepared for what was about to occur. Before Tobin adjusted his possibles bag, which hung around his neck, he retrieved two .53-caliber rifle balls and put them in his mouth. With saliva now on the lead balls, it was faster to spit the balls down the shaft of the Hawken rifle than to insert them by hand.[35]

When he was ready, Tobin resumed his advance in an attempt to ambush the men. However, the seasoned scout stepped on a stick, which broke. Hearing the crack, Felipe Espinosa jumped from his position and grabbed his pistol. Tobin recalled the following events:

Before he turned around fairly, I fired and hit him in the side; he bellowed like a bull and cried out, "Jesus favor me," and cried to his companion, "Escape. I am killed."[36]

Felipe's nephew José Vincente ran for cover in the aspen trees. Evidently, Tobin didn't have a clear shot at the desperado.

Tobin cautiously walked over to where Felipe Espinosa lay. He was mortally wounded but still alive. When Espinosa began unleashing a profanity-laced tirade at Tobin, one of the soldiers opened fire, hitting the outlaw several times. Finally, after months of bloody terror, the Espinosas were dead. Tobin described his next act:

I then caught him by the hair, drew his head back over a fallen tree and cut it off. I sent [Montoya] to cut off the head of the other fellow; he cut it off and brought it to me.[37]

An entry in the diary of Felipe Espinosa offered a motive for the widespread murderous rampage:

They ruined our family—they took everything in our house. Seeing this, we said, "We would rather be dead than see such infamies committed on our families!" But we have repented of killing. Pardon us for what we have done.[38]

On the morning of Friday, October 16, 1863, Tom Tobin, Juan Montoya and Lieutenant Baldwin's troops returned to Fort Garland. Tobin later described the event:

I rode up in front of the commanding officer's quarters and called for Col. Tappan. I rolled the assassins [sic] heads out of the sack at Col. Tappan's feet. I said, "Here, Col., I have accomplished what you wished. This head is Espinosa's. This other is his companion's head, and there is no mistake made."[39]

Years later, Tobin's grandson Christopher "Kit" Carson, in an interview with Edgar L. Hewett, a friend of Tobin's, recalled the story as told to him by his grandfather:

When arriving at Ft. Garland, the Colonel, some of his officers and their wives had been out riding. An announcement was made that Grandpa was there to see the Colonel. He was brought into a large room, where the officers and wives [were] *relaxing after their ride. Grandpa held the gunnysack upside down, rolling the heads out on the floor.* [The] *ladies were screaming; the officers and the Colonel even looked a little green. When I was very young, we lived at Ft. Garland in that room. Grandpa said that was the colonel's way of getting even for him rolling those heads out on that floor.*[40]

Colonel Tappan paid tribute to Tom Tobin's skills, as well as his soldiers, in a ceremony the following day, Saturday, October 17, 1863. Following the ceremony, Tappan encouraged Tobin to apply for the reward Governor Evans had offered. Tobin did so and spent years working through government paperwork. In the end, Tobin never received the promised award.

The day after the celebration, Tobin left the fort, bound for his home and family. For the next several years, Tobin remained at his Trinchera ranch near Costilla. In 1866, Reverend John L. Dyer, the famed "snow shoe" itinerant Methodist preacher, had extend his circuit south into the San Louis Valley. Following a sermon at Fort Garland, Reverend Dyer rode out to Tobin's ranch and asked for permission to preach there.

In September 1868, Tobin received a message from General William Penrose, asking for his assistance in a winter campaign against the Indians. Penrose further asked Tobin to report to Fort Lyon in southeastern Colorado Territory and to bring along Charles Autobees. After both Tobin and Autobees got their affairs in order, they left for the fort. Once the men arrived at the fort, they were briefed on the military expedition and issued the latest in military weaponry. Each man was outfitted with a new Spencer seven-shot carbine rifle. Tobin gave his trusty Hawken rifle to the ordnance officer for safekeeping. General William Penrose and his three hundred troops left Fort Lyon the first week of November 1868. Tom Tobin served as chief of the accompanying scouts. On November 23, the military expedition reached the Washita River in what would become Oklahoma Territory. Here, General Eugene Carr took over command of the troops from General Penrose. Unknown to General Penrose was the fact that Carr needed the troops to join Colonel George Armstrong Custer's Seventh Cavalry, which was on its way to the site. In the meantime, General Carr sent a detachment of the soldiers to Fort Lyon for more supplies. Leading the soldiers was Tom Tobin. Thus, Tobin was not present when Custer and his Seventh Cavalry annihilated Black Kettle and his Cheyenne people on the banks of the Washita River on November 27, 1868. It was almost four years to the day after the Sand Creek Massacre in Colorado Territory.

By 1873, fifty-year-old Tom Tobin had settled into a quieter lifestyle. The 1870 census showed that Tobin was quite well-off by the standards of the era. His personal wealth was listed as just under $9,000, and he owned both his Trinchera ranch and his home in Costilla.

By 1878, all of Tobin's children were married and starting their own lives. The last to marry was the Tobins' youngest daughter, fourteen-year-old Pascualita. On March 4, 1878, Pascuala married twenty-four-year-old William "Billy" Carson, the oldest son of Christopher "Kit" Carson. As with all of Tobin daughters' weddings, the ceremony took place in the Tobin home. The couple settled into Carson's ranchhouse not far from the Tobin home in Costilla County.[41] On December 13, 1879, the Carsons welcomed their first child, Josephine. Attie was born three years later. On June 30, 1883, the couple's only son, Christopher III, was born. They called him "Kit" in honor of his paternal grandfather. In 1886, Carson ran for sheriff of Costilla County and won the election. Promptly after the election, he appointed his father-in-law, Tobin, deputy sheriff.

On January 1, 1887, Pascuala Bernal Tobin died at the age of fifty-seven. A grieving Tom Tobin buried his wife of forty-three years in the small Hillside Cemetery near his home. He placed a simple marker, which listed her name and date of death, at her grave.[42]

For months, Tobin spent a good portion of every day at her grave site. Tobin's health began to deteriorate, and his ranch also began falling into disrepair. Tobin's children encouraged him to remarry, and on July 17, 1887, sixty-four-year-old Tobin married a forty-year-old widow, Maria Rosa Quintana.[43]

It was also in 1887 that William "Billy" Carson moved his family to Fort Garland, where he opened a mercantile store in one of the vacant buildings at the post. The fort had been closed since 1883, so the Carson family was able to refurbish the old commandant's quarters as their living space. As the small community around the fort continued to grow, Carson's business flourished. That all changed on May 1, 1888. On that day, Carson began drinking early in the day. As the day progressed, he and his wife, Pascualita, argued. It all ended with Carson beating his wife. When Carson finally left the house, Pascualita gathered her children and walked the three miles to her father's Trinchera ranch. She proceeded to tell her father of the argument with her husband, but her bruised face told an angered Tom Tobin all he needed to know. Tobin hitched his wagon, grabbed his pistol and knife and left in a fury for Fort Garland. Tobin arrived at the fort at approximately 4:00 p.m., his horses sweating from the three-mile run. Tobin dismounted from the wagon in front of Carson's store. Carl Wulsten was inside the store when Tom Tobin stormed through the door. The following is his eyewitness account:

> *I saw Tom Tobins [sic] come in at the door with a large Bowie knife in his hand. I looked around and saw everybody trying to get out of his way. Old Tom seemed to be in a terrible rage and fury. He went into the butcher shop and came back toward the front door when Billy Carson came in by the same. Old Tom lunged at Billy, who struck Tom right in the face. Several men rushed upon them both and separated them. Tobins went out with [the] crowd. When I turned, I looked into the barrel of a large Colt's revolver in the right hand of Tom Tobins. Billy Carson was behind the counter. He was holding a rifle in his hands. When Tobins came in, he rushed over to the counter, laid his pistol on a pile of coats and vests and fired. Billy Carson, warned by somebody crying out, "Look out there," dropped to the floor at the moment Tobins fired. Billy crept along the floor behind the counter and rushed out the front door. I ran around the building, through its yard and went to the southwest corner of the hospital building, where the Costilla County Bank room was. Peeping around the corner, I saw Tobins in front of the store, shooting at Billy Carson, who was running, Indian fashion, in a zigzag toward the old cavalry stables. Tobins emptied his revolver at him. The last shot Tobins fired came very near hitting Billy.*[44]

Tobin remained in critical condition for several weeks. Six months after Tobin's son-in-law shot him, Billy Carson himself was shot. This shooting occurred on January 18, 1889. At approximately 7:00 p.m., Carson was unhitching his wagon team when he was kicked by one of the horses. Evidently, Carson's Colt revolver was not holstered properly, as the horse's hoof hit the hammer of the gun, and the pistol fired. The bullet struck Carson in the thigh and became lodged in the back of his knee. Dr. Gale, ironically the same physician who attended his father-in-law's bullet wound, treated Carson's gunshot wound. After examining and cleaning the wound, Dr. Gale planned to do surgery to remove the bullet the following day. However, nearly eleven hours later, William "Billy" Carson suddenly died. Dr. Gale suspected tetanus, or lockjaw, as the cause of death.[45] It was an odd assumption on the part of the doctor, as tetanus is an acute infection that he apparently did not see in his one and only examination of Carson's wound. Two days later, on January 21, 1889, William Carson II was buried near his mother-in-law, Pascuala Bernal Tobin, in the Hillside Cemetery.

In time, Tobin's health improved. The mutilation of his genital area caused severe pain for the rest of his life, as did his kidneys and bladder. His pelvis never healed, and his hips weakened. As the years went on, Tobin was forced to use a cane.

Finally, in 1893, the Colorado State Senate passed Senate Bill No. 165, authorizing payment of $1,000 to Thomas Tate Tobin for the killing of the bloody Espinosas nearly thirty years earlier. Although this certainly helped Tobin in the short run, he was still heavily in debt. Two years later, Tobin sold half of his 320-acre Trinchera ranch. Four years later, he sold another 100 acres to William Myer for $1,500. For whatever reason, this did not alleviate Tobin's financial difficulties. In 1900, Tobin struck a deal with Myer. Myer would buy the remaining acreage of Tobin's Trinchera ranch for $4,200. In return, Myer would allow Tobin to live on the ranch rent-free for the rest of his life.

Although Tobin had a place to live, he had no income. That same year, Tobin applied for a government pension, claiming his many years as scout for the U.S. Army. Years of government red tape resulted in a firm denial in March 1904.

Now nearly destitute, Tobin's health rapidly declined. His eyesight was failing, and by April that year, he was nearly blind. His grandson Christopher "Kit" Carson III stayed with him and read to him every day. The two were very close, and Tobin's grandson always remembered his childhood at Fort Garland with his family and hearing the pioneer tales of his grandfather.

On the night of Sunday, May 15, 1904, as Kit was reading to his grandfather, he noticed Tobin's eyes had closed and his breathing had become shallow and labored. Kit and Rosa, Tobin's wife, managed to sit him up in an effort to improve his breathing. However, as soon as they did, blood poured from Tobin's mouth and nose. Within seconds, Thomas Tate Tobin was dead.

The next morning, as Kit and Rosa prepared Tobin's body for burial, William Myer sent a wire to Alamosa, ordering a casket and new suit for Tobin, which arrived by train that evening. The following day, May 17, 1904, Thomas Tate Tobin was buried next to his first wife, Pascuala, in the Hillside Cemetery west of Fort Garland. The original wooden cross marking Tobin's grave was later replaced by a stone marker.[46]

Years later, Tobin's grandson remarked on the friendship of both of his grandfathers. On September 10, 1946, Edgar L. Hewett, an old friend of Tom Tobin, interviewed Christopher "Kit" Carson III, the grandson of both Tom Tobin and Kit Carson. The interview took place at Carson's

A family at Fort Garland. *Public domain.*

Kit Carson's Trading Post, a business owned by the famed grandson in the town of Kit Carson, obviously named for his paternal grandfather, located in the San Luis Valley.[47]

> *Grandpa Tobin had known Grandpa Carson a long time; they both came from the same town in what is now Missouri. Grandpa Tobin was a lot younger than Grandpa Carson; he looked on him as a sort of hero. Both of my grandfathers were well respected and trusted.*

Thomas Tate Tobin, the trailblazer, scout and tracker, led a colorful life and was among the frontier pioneers of Colorado. He never thought that of himself, but history shows otherwise.

7

FORT GARLAND

he San Luis Valley of Southwestern Colorado is an enormous intermountain basin. At 7,600 feet above sea level, the valley is surrounded by Mount Blanca and the central Rockies to the north, the Sangre De Cristo Range to the northeast, the San Juan Mountain Range to the west and La Veta Pass south to New Mexico.

In 1803, with the American Louisiana Purchase from France, the San Luis Valley was still occupied by Spain. However, when President Thomas Jefferson sent Lewis and Clark west of the Missouri River and over the Rocky Mountains, passing nearly one thousand miles north of the area known as New Mexico, the Spaniards considered them trespassers. On alert for such expeditions, the military party led by Lieutenant Zebulon Montgomery Pike was arrested at the Spaniards' stockade, near the future site of Fort Garland, by Spanish authorities in January 1807.

Nevertheless, when Pike published his report of the expedition, Americans learned of the West and the San Luis Valley. Pike's route spawned a steady group of trappers and traders to travel throughout the area. This group eventually included a young mountain man by the name of Christopher "Kit" Carson, who had served as a guide for the "Pathfinder," John C. Frémont.

Following the Mexican-American War of 1846, the Treaty of Guadalupe Hidalgo was signed on February 2, 1848. The treaty stipulated that for $15 million, paid to the Mexican government, the U.S. government would receive the lands north of the Rio Grande River, including the areas of

Colorado, New Mexico and Arizona, as well as the entire area of today's states of California, Nevada and Utah.

Due to the government's westward expansion known as manifest destiny, a steady increase of travel and settlement occurred throughout the area. To protect the settlers, the government commissioned the first U.S. military post in the region.

On March 30, 1852, Commander Edwin Vose Sumner of the First U.S. Dragoons issued orders for the construction of the new fort. Sumner, a native of Boston, Massachusetts, named the military post Fort Massachusetts. Sumner appointed Major George A.H. Blake to lead Company H of the First U.S. Dragoons, as well as the Third Infantry, to build the fort.[48]

The site of the fort was strategically located in the San Luis Valley on Ute Creek. It was approximately eighty-five miles north of Taos, New Mexico, becoming the northern military command in the Department of New Mexico. The location, at the foothills of Mount Blanca, provided protection against the marauding Jicarilla Apache Indians and a guard against their approach from New Mexico by way of La Veta Pass. Under Major Blake, 120 infantrymen built the new military post, constructed of vertical logs chinked with mud and covered with flat roofs. Six buildings comprised the fort, which also included a hospital. After three months, the fort was complete. On June 22, 1852, the American flag, measuring twenty by thirty-six feet, was raised above Fort Massachusetts. However, a year into operating the new military post, General Joseph K.F. Mansfield inspected the fort and found it an inadequate means of defense. In his report, he wrote: "Fort Massachusetts is a quadrangular stockade of pine log pickets, inclosing [*sic*] comfortable quarters for 150 men, cavalry and infantry. It is too far removed from the general track of Indians to be of much service in protecting the settlements."

During the winter of 1855–56, with subzero temperatures and a lack of fresh water and proper nutrition, many soldiers were afflicted with scurvy. The following year, the U.S. government secured a twenty-five-year lease at one dollar a year from Charles Beaubien, who owned the land in the Sangre de Cristo area through a Mexican land grant.

With the signing of the lease on July 17, 1856, Brigadier General John Garland, the commander of the Ninth Military Department, issued orders for a new military post to replace the insufficient Fort Massachusetts. The location of the new fort provided an unobstructed view from every direction, lending to an excellent defense position. Situated between Trinchera and Ute Creeks, the new fort would have plenty of fresh water, something Fort Massachusetts sorely lacked.

This flagpole at Fort Garland remains to this day. *Public domain.*

The construction of the fort was carried out under the command of Captain Thomas Duncan. With his 150 soldiers of Company A, Third U.S. Infantry, local laborers were also hired. Several men worked together, digging an acequia, or water ditch, which flowed from Ute Creek to the fort area and then into Sangre de Cristo Creek.

Red adobe brick, known as territorial adobe, was used to build each of the nearly forty buildings. As stated earlier, Charles Autobees was put in charge of the adobe construction. However, a few days into the construction, a local worker by the name of Juan Pineda stabbed Autobees through his left arm and into his breast, with the blade coming close to his heart. Due to Autobees's perilous life-threatening condition, his half brother, the famed scout Tom Tobin, temporarily replaced Autobees until he was well enough to return to his duties.

When completed, the rectangular fort, consistent with military posts of the era, comprised several single-story adobe buildings, all with walls that

Soldiers' barracks at Fort Garland. *Author's collection.*

were nearly three feet thick. Strong vertical posts supported roof beams covered with sod. The infantry barracks were located on the west side, and the cavalry barracks were on the east side. On the south end were the company quarters, as well as the mess hall and blacksmith shop. The garrison's commandant and officers' quarters were located on the north end. Fort Garland could accommodate two companies of one hundred men each and seven officers. The sally port, or gated entrance, located on the east end, opened to a large parade ground. In the center was a flag pole. On June 24, 1858, during a military ceremony, the American flag was lowered at Fort Massachusetts for the last time. Carrying the flag in a six-mile march to the site of the new fort were members of Company E, U.S. Regiment of Mounted Rifles. There, the large flag was raised up the new flag pole, which still stands today.

A few years later, westward traveler W.H. Rideing remarked on seeing the fort for the first time:

> We obtained a glimpse of our destination—a rectangular group of brick-red adobe buildings, flat-roofed, squat, and together dispiriting in their unmitigated ugliness, with the United States flag clinging to a central staff. The mountain ranges encircle a horribly unvaried desert of the plain. It is positively distracting in its monotony. We wonder how a man can look upon it from day to day without yielding to the overwhelming sense of oppressiveness that it is prone to communicate. And when we are well within the walls of the fort, we are struck with the immediate commiseration for all the unfortunate officers and men condemned to live in so desolate a place.[49]

Fort Garland was the center of many frontier episodes in Colorado's early history. With the outbreak of the Civil War, soldiers at Fort Garland played an important role in one of the few battles fought in the West. The fort served as an enlistment site for Colorado volunteers. These volunteers were mustered in as Companies A and B of the Second Colorado Infantry Volunteers. Early in 1862, they marched from Fort Garland, south into New Mexico, under the command of Major John M. Chivington. The Battle of Glorieta Pass, led by Chivington and the Colorado volunteers, destroyed the Confederate attempt to gain control of Union supplies, including gold. Chivington, praised for this victory, would later be condemned by a Congressional hearing following the Sand Creek Massacre two years later.

Colonel Samuel F. Tappan, who served alongside Chivington at the Battle of Glorieta Pass, became commander of Fort Garland in July 1863. Almost

This page and opposite: Around Fort Garland. *Library of Congress.*

immediately, Tappan's soldiers were sent to arrest the Espinosa brothers, Felipe and Vivian, who had been committing crimes in the area, from horse stealing to murder. The attempted arrest by the soldiers turned into a shootout, with the Espinosa brothers escaping unscathed. (See Tom Tobin chapter.) On October 11, 1863, Tom Tobin met with Colonel Sam Tappan, who personally selected Tobin to track down the murderous Espinosa Gang. Tobin accepted the assignment and left the fort the following day. When Tobin returned to the fort five days later, he again met with Tappan, telling him he had completed his assignment satisfactorily. As proof, Tobin opened his burlap sack, and the heads of two Espinosas rolled onto the ground at Tappan's feet.

The increase of population made the Native Americans, particularly the Ute bands of the area, hostile. As the Ute raids in the San Luis Valley intensified, General John Pope of Fort Union wrote a recommendation to General William Tecumseh Sherman in August 1866.

Carson accepted General Sherman's appointment as commander of Fort Garland on May 19, 1866. Through his years of dealing with the Utes, Carson knew their language and had become friends with many, including Ute chief Ouray. General Sherman personally met with Carson at the fort in September 1866 to discuss treaties with the Utes. "His integrity is simply perfect," Sherman later wrote. Because of their friendship and trust, Ouray brought his band of Utes to Fort Garland, where he and Carson worked together to negotiate peace. Because of Carson, peace with the Utes lasted for the next decade in the San Luis Valley.

Fort Garland soldiers' graves. *Photograph by O.T. Davis, 1908; public domain.*

Fort Garland.
*Photograph by
O.T. Davis, circa
1905–10; public
domain.*

The Ninth Cavalry of the famed Black buffalo soldiers were stationed at Fort Garland from 1876 to 1879. These soldiers were instrumental in the mediation of many conflicts between the Utes and white settlers, including the aftermath of the Meeker Massacre, as well as skirmishes between the Utes and gold miners in the San Juan Mountains.

Fort Garland was officially closed by the U.S. Army in November 1883. Following the fort's closure, Kit Carson's son William ran a store in the old hospital building. A local businessman, William Meyer, bought the property in 1915. He lived in the commandant's quarters, where Kit Carson had lived forty years earlier. Meyer died there in 1923.

The Colorado Historical Society bought the property in 1945, and after an extensive restoration, it was opened to the public as a museum in 1950. Today, five of the original buildings form the basis of the fort museum. Reconstructed buildings complete the fort museum experience. The nucleus of the fort is the original parade ground, complete with the 1858 flagpole.

8

JIM BECKWOURTH

A ROCKY MOUNTAIN LEGEND

J im Beckworth: mountain man, scout, frontiersman, honorary Indian chief and the first to pen an autobiography—and what a story it was. He was legendary in his own time, although early historians largely discounted him.

James Pierson Beckwourth was born on April 26, 1798, in Fredericksburg, Frederick County, Virginia. His mother was an enslaved house worker.[50] His father, Sir Jennings Beckwourth, an officer during the Revolutionary War, was the owner of a large plantation. Unconventional for the times, Beckwourth raised young Jim as his own son, although, according to the law, Jim was legally considered enslaved. His father appeared in open court on three separate occasions and "acknowledged the execution of a Deed of Emancipation from him to James, a mulatto boy."[51]

When young Beckwourth was of age, his father sent him to Saint Louis for his education. Beckwourth later related:

> *When about ten years of age, I was sent to Saint Louis to attend school, where I continued until the year 1812. I was then apprenticed to a man in Saint Louis named George Casner to learn the trade of blacksmith. I took to the trade with some unwillingness at first, but becoming reconciled to it, I was soon much pleased with my occupation. When I attained my nineteenth year, my sense of importance had considerably expanded, and, like many others of my age, I felt my self [sic] already quite a man. One morning, I was assailed by my principal in language, which I considered*

James Beckworth. *Public domain.*

unduly harsh and insulting, and on his threatening to dismiss me, I attempted to to reply and acknowledge that his doing so would exactly square with my wishes. Provoked at this, he seized a hammer and flung it at me. I dodged the missile and threw it back at him.

Not long after this episode, Beckwourth saw an advertisement in the February 13, 1822 issue of the *Missouri Gazette*, recruiting young men to join William Ashley's Mountain Fur Company: "To enterprising young men. The subscriber wishes to engage one hundred men, to ascend the river Missouri to its source, there to be employed for one, two or three years. For particulars, enquire of Major Andrew Henry or to the subscriber at Saint Louis. Wm. H. Ashley."

It was an opportunity for adventure that the young strong-willed Beckwourth dreamed of. Beckwourth recalled:

Accordingly, I went home to my father and related the difficulty with my master. Seeing my determination, my father finally consented to my departure. He admonished me with some wholesome precepts, gave me five hundred dollars cash, together with a good horse, saddle, and bridle, and bade me Godspeed upon my journey.

With the blessing of his father, Beckwourth signed on with the Rocky Mountain Fur Company. Beckwourth would be counted among the future legendary members of the company, including James Bridger, Thomas Fitzpatrick, David Jackson, Hugh Glass, Jedediah Smith and William Sublette. Beckwourth's first duties with the fur company were to attend to the horses along the westward trail. It was during this time that he was able to practice his marksmanship and also learn the skills of hunting, trapping and scouting.

Beckwourth was fortunate to work directly under Ashley during those formidable years of fur trading. Ashley's new trading company was the first to depend primarily on trapping beavers rather than buying them from Native Americans. Thus, Ashley conceived of the idea of holding a large open trading arena for trappers and Indians. That first year, 1825, Ashley selected a spot near Henry's Fork on the Green River in today's southwestern Wyoming. Here, Ashley and his men convened along a small stream.

So successful was this first rendezvous that Ashley named the small stream Rendezvous Creek. From then on, the mountain man rendezvous became an annual event. Beckwourth was present at that first gathering, where over one hundred mountain men traded beaver pelts and purchased supplies for the next season. The event marked a celebrated era in American history. It was also during this time that Beckwourth became acquainted with other well-known mountain men, such as Christopher "Kit" Carson, Thomas Fitzpatrick, Jim Bridger, Jedediah Smith and William Sublette, to name a few. In the fall of 1828, while trapping in the high Rocky Mountains along the Powder River with Jim Bridger, Beckwourth came into contact with a party of Crow Indians. After some conversation and trading, Beckwourth concluded that he could make more money trapping and trading with the Crow Indians than he had made working for William Ashley, Smith or Sublette. Beckwourth terminated his employment with them and camped with the Crow tribe along the river. Beckwourth spent the next four years with the Crow.

In 1832, a representative of the American Fur Company, Kenneth McKenzie, persuaded Beckwourth to join his company as a company agent among the Crow Indians. Beckwourth agreed and spent the next five years with the tribe. During this time, he gained considerable influence among the Crow people. By their very nature and reputation, the Crow were aggressive in protecting their lands and were fierce in battle. Beckwourth's autobiography is replete with accounts of his fighting abilities and bravery on the battlefield. However, while these tales are largely unconfirmed, it stands to reason that no outsider could have stayed with such a warrior society without distinguishing himself in battle.

It was during this time that Beckwourth, by his own account, was smitten with a young Crow warrior woman, Pine Leaf. According to Beckwourth, Pine Leaf and her twin brother were captured by the Crow when she approximately ten years old and were raised by Crow women. When her brother was killed in a battle with the Blackfeet, Pine Leaf swore that she would kill one hundred enemy warriors with her own hands. Pine Leaf was allowed to participate in may battles fought by the Crow, and her bravery was greatly admired.

Beckwourth courted Pine Leaf in the traditional Crow custom, and in time, Pine Leaf agreed to marry him "when the pine leaves turn yellow,"

Green River rendezvous. *Alfred Jacob Miller, circa 1858–60; public domain.*

Beckwourth later related. Pine Leaf continued this evasive game with Beckwourth for some time before finally relenting. The couple were married in the Crow tradition for only five weeks before Beckwourth left the Crow encampment. He never saw Pine Leaf again. Perhaps Beckwourth won the evasive game Pine Leaf started.

In 1837, Beckwourth attended the annual rendezvous at Green River and Horse Creek. This was Beckwourth's last mountain man rendezvous. Following the rendezvous, Beckwourth took his beaver pelts to Saint Louis, Missouri, for trade. While he was there, he began to seek better employment opportunities.

As luck would have it—something Beckwourth seemed to have plenty of—he ran into his trapper friends Andrew Sublette and Louis Vasquez. Vasquez told Beckwourth of the Bent brothers and their monopoly on trade with the westward travelers and Indians along the Arkansas River in southern Colorado. Vasquez, an experienced Colorado trader himself, told Beckwourth that his experience with the Indian people would be of great service at Bent's Fort in Colorado.

Beckwourth accompanied Louis Vasquez west to Fort Vasquez, located near the South Platte River. Vasquez was glad to have his services, and Beckwourth was named "agent-in-charge." Beckwourth successfully established himself among the Cheyenne and became well respected. He remained there, trading with the Cheyenne during that winter. Due in large part to Beckwourth's communication skills with the Cheyenne, Vasquez had a successful fall and winter trade at the fort, making a handsome profit that not only satisfied their debts but also made enough to carry through the next trading season. Nevertheless, Beckwourth set out for Bent's Fort along the Santa Fe Trail. He had made his mark with the American Fur Company, which had successfully captured the fur trade market in the upper Missouri River region, based at Saint Louis. Now, Beckwourth hoped to be a part of Charles and William Bent's trading enterprise, where they had a monopoly along the Arkansas River and south into Mexico.

Beckwourth's trading skills with the Cheyenne and Arapaho were soon apparent to the Bent brothers. Not only did he form a lifelong friendship with Charles and William, but Beckwourth also formed lasting relations with the Arapaho and Cheyenne who frequented the fort, including Black Kettle. Beckwourth's skill with Indian negotiations, as well as his friendship and loyalty to the Bents, enhanced their peaceful existence along the Arkansas River.

However, the following year, Beckwourth left the fort and moved to an establishment upstream on the Arkansas River known as Fort Pueblo. Here, he continued to trade with Indians and local settlers. It was during this time that Beckwourth married a local woman, Luisa Sandoval. In October 1845,

Arkansas River. *Roy Luck (CC BY 2.0).*

Beckwourth and his wife relocated to Taos, New Mexico, where his former employer Charles Bent now lived. While Charles Bent went into politics, becoming the first territorial governor of New Mexico, Beckwourth operated a successful trading post and hotel.

In 1847, with the Mexican-American War in full force, Taos was a boiling pot of hostility. The Mexican Revolt of 1847 erupted in Taos. Militants from the Mexican faction invaded the town, burning homes and buildings and terrorizing citizens. Although Governor Charles Bent pleaded for calm, the violence turned to murder, and the murderers turned toward the governor. When Beckwourth learned of the murderous plot on the governor, he hurried through the burning streets to help his friend. He was too late. Nearly three hundred Mexican revolters had stormed the home of Governor Bent and shot him in the head. Realizing Bent was not dead, they then beheaded him in front of his daughter.

After the murder of Charles Bent, Beckwourth left New Mexico. In 1850, returning to his love of scouting, Beckwourth and his party ventured west toward California. Traveling through the Sierra Nevada Mountain Range, Beckwourth spotted a pass through the area, which he later described as "far away to the southward that seemed lower than any other. We proceeded in an easterly direction, and all busied themselves in searching for gold; but my errand was of a different character: I had come to discover what I suspected to be a pass that would afford the best wagon road into the American Valley approaching from the east."

A year later, Beckwourth had developed the trail through the Sierra Nevadas, now known as Beckwourth Pass. Its lower elevation spared the settlers and gold prospectors from the several steep grades and high passes of other routes, such as the Donner Pass. For nearly a decade, Beckwourth remained in the mountains, exploring and scouting for various companies.

By 1858, Beckwourth and Louis Vasquez had formed a new partnership. In early 1860, the two opened a mercantile store in Denver City. While Beckwourth operated the store, Vasquez made periodic trips to Saint Louis for trade goods, such as crockery, dry goods, dried fruit, nails and window glass.[52]

Within a few years, the mercantile enterprise was doing so well that Beckwourth expanded the business by taking wagons loaded with goods to various forts, including Bent's Fort. Because of his friendship with the Arapaho and Cheyenne, Beckwourth also served as a peacemaker of sorts.

It so happened that during one of his return trips from Bent's Fort, Beckwourth was at Fort Lyon on November 28, 1864, when Colonel John Chivington arrived unannounced. Placing the fort on lockdown, Chivington said little regarding his presence, only that the soldiers were to be ready to march before daylight the following morning. Chivington forced sixty-two-year-old Beckwourth and Robert Bent to be his guides. During the early morning march over frozen ground and in freezing temperatures, Beckwourth collapsed and fell off his horse. When Beckwourth had somewhat recovered, he was lifted back on his horse, and a reluctant Robert Bent was ordered to guide Chivington's men to the Cheyenne village along Sand Creek, where many of his relatives were camped. Just after dawn on the morning of November 29, 1864, Chivington led a surprise attack on the village that became a massacre of innocent men, women and children. Jim Beckwourth witnessed the atrocity, including the murder of a prisoner, the interpreter John Smith's son Jack.

Following what became known as the Sand Creek Massacre, several local, state and military investigations were held. Beckwourth's testimony during the government trials concerning the actions of Chivington led to Beckwourth's appointment by the U.S. government as an advisory toward peace negotiations with the Indians.

Two years later, in the fall of 1866, Beckwourth led a military column out of Fort Laramie to a Crow camp in Montana Territory. He was acting as an emissary on behalf of the U.S. Army in an effort to begin negotiations between the Crow and the government. During the trip, Beckwourth became ill, suffering from severe headaches and nosebleeds.

Perhaps quite fitting, given his many years living among the Crow, James Pierson Beckwourth died in the Montana camp of the Crow people on October 29, 1866. Out of respect for the frontier pioneer, Beckwourth's wrapped body was placed on a platform in a tree, in accordance to Crow tradition.

Thus ended the adventures of James P. Beckwourth, Colorado's first Black pioneer frontiersman.

9

FORT VASQUEZ

Located on the northern plains, Fort Vasquez was an important trading post for trappers and Indians alike.

Pierre Luis Vasquez was born on October 3, 1798, to Benito Andres and Marie Julie Papin Vasquez of Saint Louis, Missouri. Benito had arrived in America in 1769 from Galicia, Spain, with a detail of the Spanish army. Their mission was to establish forts along the Mississippi River. Years later, his son would follow in his footsteps.

At the age of twenty-five, Pierre Luis, by this time known as Louis, struck out on his own. After spending a few years trading with the Pawnee, Vasquez partnered with a group of mountain men, trapping and trading in the Rocky Mountain West. Vasquez, who spoke five languages as well as many Indian dialects, quickly became very popular, earning the nickname "Old Vaskiss" from his colleagues. Louis Vasquez attended the annual rendezvous of 1833 and 1834 at the confluence of Green River and Horse Creek in an area that would later become Sublette County, Wyoming.

It was during this time that Vasquez met a fellow trader also from Saint Louis, Missouri, twenty-seven-year-old Andrew Sublette, one of the five famed Sublette brothers. Their parents, originally from Kentucky, had moved their large family to Saint Louis in 1817, and there, they owned and operated a tavern.

Following the rendezvous, due to fierce competition, several of the fur trading companies either dissolved or changed hands. Louis Vasquez and Andrew Sublette formed their own partnership. In the fall of 1835, the two had located a site near the South Platte River on the northern plains of today's Weld County, Colorado. There, the two set about building a trading post. Fort Vasquez was strategically located between Fort Laramie in Wyoming and Bent's Fort along the Arkansas River in today's Southern Colorado. The position of the fort marked a halfway point along what was known as the Trapper's Trail.

The fort was constructed on a low plateau, and Mexican laborers were hired to build the adobe complex fashioned after Bent's Fort. Inside the square fort, its

Pierre Louis Vasquez. *Public domain.*

interior rooms included sleeping quarters, a blacksmith shop and a trading room kitchen.

Fort Vasquez soon became an active trading post for traders as well as the Arapaho and Cheyenne tribes in the area. It was here that James Beckwourth came into the employ of Louis Vasquez. With Beckwourth's extraordinary trading skills among the Indians, he successfully established himself among the Cheyenne and became well respected, and Vasquez appointed Beckwourth "agent-in-charge."

Due in large part to Beckwourth's communication skills with the Arapaho and Cheyenne, Vasquez and Sublette had a successful fall and winter trade at the fort, making a handsome profit that not only satisfied their debts but also made them enough money to carry them through the next trading season.

However, the success was short-lived. Due to the decline of the fur trade and falling prices, Vasquez and Sublette sold their enterprise to the Locke and Randolph Company in 1841. This new company had very little success, and after an Indian attack, the fort was abandoned.

During the gold rush era, the fort was was rebuilt in 1860. For the next few years, Fort Vasquez served as a stop along the Overland Trail.

In 1932, with the assistance of a federal grant through the Works Progress Administration (WPA), an archaeology group began the tedious task of finding the original stockade walls. Two years later, the owners of the property, Ethel Hoffman and Pearl Perdiew, donated an acre of

Top: South Platte River, near old Fort Saint Vrain, Colorado. *Photo by William Henry Jackson, ca. 1882-1900. Public Domain.*

Bottom: Fort Vasquez. *Photograph by John Stanton, Fortwiki (CC BY-SA 3.0).*

the land to the Weld County Commissioners. Work continued with local volunteers until 1935. The following year, crews with the WPA rebuilt the fort in accordance with the original wall foundation. The original adobe bricks found at the site were used for the walls, as well as the guard towers, firing ledges and portals. However, due to conflicts with the government's right-of-way for U.S. Highway 85, the reconstructed fort is a bit shorter than the original.

Opposite, top: Fort Vasquez gate, 2007. *Charles M. Sauer, GNU Free Documentation License.*

Opposite, bottom: Fort Vasquez entrance. *Loco Steve, Flickr (CC BY-SA 3.0).*

Right: Fort Vasquez, south wall interior. *Photograph by John Stanton, Fortwiki (CC BY-SA 3.0).*

The Colorado Historical Society obtained title to the land in 1960. Colorado State University students participated in a formal excavation of the area. The two-year project, conducted from 1968 to 1970, yielded over four thousand artifacts and established the original dimensions of the fort as one hundred feet by ninety-eight and a half feet. They were also able to locate the interior wall foundations for the rooms and fireplaces.

Today, the reconstructed fort is operated as a museum.

10

EL PUEBLO

The confluence of the Arkansas River and Fountain Creek, some sixty miles upstream from Bent's Fort, had long been an area favored by Indian hunting parties and early Spanish explorers. The site was a natural crossroads for the area's many Indian tribes, Spanish soldiers, mountain men, trappers and traders. In 1806, Lieutenant Zebulon Pike and his men built what is believed to be the first structure in the area, near today's city of Pueblo. A small picket stockade became the base camp Lieutenant Pike used for his government exploration of the area and his failed attempt at climbing the looming mountain that would later bear his name. Later, French trappers recorded a series of visits to the area where they found the old stockade.

During the 1830s and 1840s, when fur trading was at its zenith, the area's trappers, scouts and Indians often camped at the confluence of the two waterways, an area the French fur trappers called Bijou Basin. It became the major stop to and from Bent's new fort, which was built downstream in 1833. When George Simpson passed through in 1841, he found the area to his liking and stayed. The following year, Simpson, with partners J.B. Doyle and Alexander Barclay, built a trading post they called El Pueblo on the site. The adobe quadrangle had eight-foot-high walls topped with picket fencing and small bastions; it was "a wretched species of fort," wrote Francis Parkman following his visit in 1846.

El Pueblo was a indeed a crude structure. Its ceiling was supported by rough logs with protruding edges, used to hang clothing and dry chili peppers and

El Pueblo. *Photograph by John Stanton, Fortwiki (CC BY-SA 3.0).*

Indian corn. The interior walls were plastered with adobe, whitewashed and covered with sheepskin. The floors were made of the area's soil, sprinkled with water twice daily and swept until an eventual hard dirt crust formed. The rooms were small, ten feet square, with no beds. Three to five people slept on the floors in blanket rolls in each room. The food was cooked and served on the floor, which was spread with blankets.

A corral for horses was erected near the fort, while cattle grazed below the fort along the river. The men of the fort tended the livestock and worked with traders and Indians. The women spent their days cooking and sewing.

El Pueblo was a busy place. As the only trading post in the Upper Arkansas Valley, it soon became a cultural crossroads. Here, Mexican families came to trade and settled in the area. Local Indian tribes, such as the Arapaho, Cheyenne, Utes and Jicarilla Apaches came to trade, as did many frontiersmen of the era. James Beckwourth was one of those traders who came to Fort Pueblo, as several of the frontiersmen called the trading post. Beckwourth stayed at the fort for two years while he continued to trade with Indians and local settlers. After marrying a local woman, Luisa Sandoval, Beckwourth left Fort Pueblo in October 1845.

Other frontiersmen passed through the fort, including Christopher "Kit" Carson, "Uncle" Dick Wootton and George Frederick Ruxton, who spent part of the winter of 1847 at Fort Pueblo. Ruxton later wrote of the experience:

> *We struck the Arkansa* [sic] *at the little Indian trading-fort of the "Pueblo," which is situated on the left bank, a few hundred yards above the mouth of the Fontaine-qui-buille, or Boiling Spring River, so-called from two springs of mineral water near its headwaters under Pike's Peak,*

Left: El Pueblo front gate. *Photograph by John Stanton, Fortwiki (CC BY-SA 3.0).*

Below: El Pueblo, interior. El Pueblo, exterior. *Photograph by John Stanton, Fortwiki (CC BY-SA 3.0).*

about sixty miles from its mouth. Here, I was hospitably entertained in the lodge. I turned my animals loose and allowed them to seek for themselves the best pastures. In the immediate vicinity of the fort, game is very scarce, and the buffalo have, within a few years, deserted the neighboring prairies, but they are always found in the mountain valleys, particularly in one called Bayou Salado, which abounds in every species of game, including elk, bear, deer, bighorn or Rocky Mountain sheep, buffalo, antelope, etc. Shortly after my arrival on Arkansa [sic], *and during a spell of fine sunny weather, I started with a Pueblo hunter for a load or two of buffalo-meat, intending to hunt on the waters of the platte and the bayou, where bulls remain in good condition during the winter months, feeding on the rich grass of the mountain valleys.*

In 1849, the U.S. government and the Ute Indians entered into a peace treaty, which Kit Carson was instrumental in securing. Unfortunately, local members of the Apache, as well as a few renegade Ute bands, were unhappy with the treaty.

For the next few years, due to an onslaught of westward migration, the local Indians, primarily Utes and Jicarilla Apaches, grew tired of their inability to stop the foreigners from invading their land. The wildlife, particularly the spirited buffalo, were disappearing, causing hardship, starvation and frustration. Thus, in the spring of 1854, disgruntled warriors began raiding along the few settlements of the upper Arkansas River. However, as winter settled in, the frontier around Fort Pueblo once again became quiet. Trading continued as Joseph Doyle arrived with two wagonloads of goods to sell just one week before Christmas.

Benito Sandoval and his son had left the day before, headed for Bent's Fort with a wagon loaded with goods to sell. Dick Wootton and a party of hunters were headed toward Fort Pueblo on December 23. At Coal Creek, the groups met, and Wootton noticed a large gathering of Indian warriors. After arriving at the fort, he learned the warriors had been seen in the area. Advising the inhabitants of the fort to stay inside, he and his group left to sound the alarm and to gather additional men to defend the fort.

Christmas Eve 1854 at Fort Pueblo was a joyous evening filled with card games and a feast of wild game, potatoes and corn. For the inhabitants of the fort, it was the last night they or anyone, for that matter, would ever spend in the fort.

The Christmas Eve celebration proceeded without care while a few of the men did keep a lookout. The party broke up just before daylight on Christmas Day 1854. Guero Pais left the fort on horseback, traveling just beyond the ford of the Fountain Creek, where he saw the band of Indian warriors that had been spotted in the area. Reporting the fact to nearby farmer Marcelino Baca, Pais raced back to the fort to give warning, and then he ran to the corrals to check the horses. There, he hid, as the warriors, led by Ute leader Tierra Blanca, thundered down the hill. After a grueling five hours of hiding, Baca determined it was safe to venture to the fort. Along the way, he came across the body of José Ignacio Valencia on the east side of the Fountain Creek. After crossing the creek, he was met by a staggering Juan Rafael Medina. As Medina clutched his belly, his blood began spilling as he soon collapsed and died. As Valencia approached the fort, two more men were found dead, arrows protruding from their bodies. At the gate of the fort, the horror continued. Three men lay dead. The courtyard of Fort Pueblo was deathly still as Baca and his rescue party of three entered. On the bloodied earthen floor lay the bodies of three men. In an another room, a father and son were found dead, along with two Ute Indians. Behind the fort, four men were found dead from arrows and gunshot wounds.

The remainder of that Christmas Day was spent burying the dead. It seemed to never end, as two more bodies were found near the river. That night, a wake was held at the home of Marcelino Baca. The fort was never again occupied.

In time, as settlers established ranches, homes and businesses in the area, a new community simply called Pueblo was created. As the new town grew, the old fort disappeared, as structures were built over the ruins.

"Uncle" Dick Wootton was an early trader in El Pueblo. *History Colorado; public domain.*

In 1989, Dr. William Buckles of the University of Southern Colorado began an archaeological survey of the original site of El Pueblo. The excavation centered on a piece of land in the heart of downtown Pueblo. Here, evidence of the adobe foundation was unearthed. The following year, the El Pueblo Museum was opened near the original site, at the corner of First Street and Union Avenue.

GEORGE BENT

A MAN AMONG TWO CULTURES

G eorge Bent, the son of a famed frontiersman and a respected Cheyenne woman, would live his life among two cultures, surviving two white men's wars. Throughout his life, he would be forced by either necessity or social pressure to choose between the white man's world or that of the Native Americans. For Bent, it was never an easy choice, nor was it ever a definitive choice. He would strike back at the white man's encroachment on his Cheyenne people's land as a distinguished member of the Cheyenne dog soldiers. In the end, George Bent would realize the future of his Cheyenne people would be secured in peace rather than in war.

George Bent was born on July 7, 1843, at the most popular trading post in the western frontier: Bent's Fort. He was the second son of William Bent and Owl Woman. George's father had established the fort on the Arkansas River in 1833. George's mother was the daughter of Tall Woman and White Thunder, the keeper of the Cheyenne Sacred Medicine Arrows. Therefore, from the time he was born, George Bent was part of two worlds. George lived with his mother's tribe in a small tipi village near his father's fort. Because of his father's trading post and his time spent living with the Cheyenne, George grew up among many ethnicities. By the time George was ten years old, he could speak fluent English, as well as the Cheyenne, Arapaho, French, Spanish, Comanche and Kiowa languages.

Years later, George related much of his life story to George E. Hyde through interviews and a long series of letters beginning in 1904. Of his early childhood, Bent wrote:

There were four children, all born at the old fort, from the marriage of my father and mother about 1835. Mary was born January 22, 1838, Robert about 1840. I was born July 7, 1843, and Julia was born in 1847. Our mother died at Julia's birth, and sometime later, our father married her younger sister, Yellow Woman. By this second marriage, there was only one child, my half-brother Charles. We were a large family at the old fort, and something was always going on. My uncle Charles stayed at the fort off and on a good deal, but his home was at Taos. Sometime after 1840, my uncles Robert and George, whom I was named for, came to the fort to live. Robert died there in 1847 and George about a year later.[53]

As a boy, George Bent spent time with his mother's people, who camped not far from Bent's Fort. Among them, he learned what all Indian boys learned: how to ride horses, how to hunt and how to learn about and study nature. He also spent considerable time at his father's fort, where he learned about commerce and how to read and write.

According to Bent's writings, in 1853, his father sent his five children to Westport, Missouri, his home state, for a proper education. Bent was at school in Missouri when the Civil War broke out.

He enlisted in the war effort and saw action at Pea Ridge. Later, he was captured by the enemy and sent to prison. His brother Robert negotiated for his release. George then returned to Colorado. For the next year, Bent lived with his father and stepmother at the trading post along the Purgatoire River. In the spring of 1863, Bent left his father and joined his younger half brother, Charley, who was living with the Cheyenne along the Arkansas River.

Meanwhile, on April 4, 1864, a few cattle herders in the employ of the freighting firm of Irwin, Jackson and Company rushed to Denver City to report the theft of nearly 175 head of cattle from their pasture at Bijou Creek. The men stated the attack was carried out by Indians, specifically implicating it was the Cheyenne. George Bent had a different view of the incident:

Some of the Cheyenne were out hunting when they came upon some of the oxen. As they did not know to whom the animals belonged, they drove them to the camp, intending to keep them until someone should lay claim to them. A day or two later, the herders went into Camp Weld at Denver and reported that Indians had run off the entire herd of oxen. I never believed this story and do not believe it now. The Indians had no use for the oxen; there

[were] *plenty of buffalo on the range that winter, and the Indians never would eat "tame meat" when they could get buffalo. Besides, I have talked to many men who were* [a part of] *these two Cheyenne camps; all denied that the oxen were stolen, and I knew they told the truth. It was not an uncommon thing for herders who let their herds stray off or get stampeded to tell the boss that Indians had run off the animals.*

Whether the Cheyenne men's account was true or Bent was simply covering for his people will never be known. What this incident does bear out is the fact that the two cultures did not and never would, with few exceptions, understand each other.

Nevertheless, Colonel Chivington ordered Lieutenant George S. Eayre, commander of the Independent Battery of Colorado Volunteer Artillery, to recover the stolen livestock. Traveling slowly through a spring snowstorm, Eayre eventually crossed the divide between the valleys of the South Platte and Arkansas Rivers, camping at Sand Creek. From there, the troops traveled along the creek to the east, where they came upon the Cheyenne villages of Coon and Crow Chief, which were camped on the Republican River. The Indians, who observed the military approach, abandoned their camp. Eayre and his men recovered a few head of the stolen cattle. The troops returned to Denver City for more supplies and returned to the area a few weeks later. Eayre and his fifty-four troops were indeed well supplied with two twelve-pound howitzers.

This was the beginning of a series of Indian raids and military counterattacks that eventually led to the massacre at Sand Creek six months later. Major Edward Wynkoop, the commander of Fort Lyon, had worked extensively with Black Kettle in an effort to negotiate peace between the two cultures. In the fall of 1864, after one of these meetings, Black Kettle agreed to release hostages in his camp in return for a peace council with Territorial Governor John Evans. Major Wynkoop firmly believed that Evans, who also served as the superintendent of Indian affairs, would welcome the opportunity to settle a peace agreement with the peaceful leaders of the Southern Cheyenne and Arapaho tribes. He was sorely mistaken.

Upon hearing that Wynkoop was on his way to Denver with a group of peaceful Indians, on September 26, Chivington wired a message to General Curtis at Fort Leavenworth. His irritation was clear and was passed on to the governor as well. Thus, the official tone for the meeting was set by Chivington and carried through by Governor Evans. The peace council, held on September 28, 1864, was presided over by a reluctant Governor

Black Kettle's (*seated behind Wynkoop, kneeling on left*) village was attacked, despite his peaceful intentions with the white man. *Denver Public Library.*

Evans. He asked several questions of the Indian leaders, including Black Kettle and White Antelope, regarding their involvement in the recent Indian uprisings. While most charges were denied, Black Kettle did present four hostages in an effort to make peace. Chivington would have none of it.

Following the Camp Weld Council, Black Kettle and White Antelope returned to their camps and prepared their people to move to Fort Lyon as Chivington had instructed. They were alarmed to find that their friend Major Wynkoop had been replaced by Major Scott Anthony. Anthony told the Indians that he believed in Wynkoop's policy. Therefore, he immediately issued rations. He further suggested that Black Kettle and Left Hand move their people to Sand Creek, approximately forty miles northeast of Fort Lyon. Anthony assured them that they would be safe there and under the military's protection. Medicine Water and Mo-chi were among those camped with Black Kettle at Sand Creek. Their great-grandson John L. Sipes, a tribal historian, wrote:

> The Cheyenne call Sand Creek, "Bo-no." In Cheyenne, this means dry creek, no water. The old ones say there was no water in there.

Meanwhile, two days after the Camp Weld meeting, Chivington received a wired message from General Curtis. The message was dated September 28, 1864, and Chivington must have been very pleased with his superior's response, as he received a message regarding the "bad Indians." This chilling military order would soon be put in motion by Colonel Chivington, resulting in death and destruction and leaving behind the bloodiest pages in the annals of Colorado history.

George Bent and his brother Charley were with Black Kettle's band.

Dawn broke cold and damp over the barren frozen prairie along the banks of Sand Creek as fog danced with the early sunrise on Tuesday, November 29, 1864. Camped in the ravine near the creek were some six hundred Indians, primarily women and children, along with chiefs Little Raven, White Antelope, Left Hand and Black Kettle.

Chivington moved his troops into position just south of the Indian camp along the banks of Sand Creek. The four twelve-pound mountain howitzers were also moved into position. As the sun rose, Chivington's troops began their charge into the sleepy Indian village, a fight that would last over six hours. George Bent later recalled:

Out of a clear blue sky, the great blow was struck. At dawn on the morning of November 29, I was still in bed when I heard shouts and the noise of the people running about the camp. I jumped up and ran out of my lodge. I looked toward the chief's lodge and saw that Black Kettle had a large American flag tied to the end of a long lodge pole and was standing in front of his lodge, holding the pole, with the flag fluttering in the gray light of the winter dawn. The Indians all began running, but they did not seem to know what to do or where to run. I ran to my lodge and got my weapons, then rushed out and joined a passing group of middle-aged Cheyenne men. We ran up the dry creek with the cavalry following us, one company on each bank, keeping right after us and firing all the time. Many of the people preceded us up the creek, and the dry bed of the stream was now a terrible sight: men, women, and children lying thickly scattered on the sand, some dead and the rest too badly wounded to move. We ran about two miles up the creek, I think, and then came to a place where the banks were very high and steep. Here, a large body of Indians had stopped under the shelter of the banks, and the older men and women had dug holes or pits under the banks, in which the people were now hiding. Just as our party reached this point, I was struck in the hip by a bullet and knocked down; but I managed to tumble into one of the holes and lay there among the warriors, women,

and children. Here, the troops kept us besieged until darkness came on.
Most of us who were hiding in the pits had been wounded before we could
reach this shelter; and there we lay all that bitter cold day from early in the
morning until almost dark, with the soldiers all around us, keeping up a
heavy fire most of the time.

The soldiers left the sandpit area and returned south to the village and the rest of Chivington's army. Chivington then assembled his troops in an area nearby and ordered his men to set up camp at the bloody site of the Indian village. Chivington knew that many of the Arapaho and Cheyenne had escaped death and destruction, fleeing in a northeastern direction toward refuge with the Cheyenne dog soldiers camped at the Smoky Hill River. Therefore, Chivington placed soldiers on alert throughout the night in case warriors should move from the Smoky Hill camp to strike in revenge.

A few hours after sundown, the remaining Cheyenne who were sheltered in the sandpits, including George Bent and Black Kettle, felt it was safe to make their way north to the Smoky Hill camp under the cloak of darkness. After a few days of rest, a band of Cheyenne dog soldiers arrived to lead the survivors to a large Sioux camp on the Solomon River and then on to Cherry Creek, a tributary that flows into the South Fork of the Republican River in Kansas Territory. Here, the injured were able to receive attention for their injuries, rest and recuperate. Meanwhile, anger over the massacre of the Cheyenne people spread like wildfire throughout the Indian societies, and the traditional war pipe was sent out by runners to all the Indian camps. All smoked the war pipe and declared war, including the dog soldiers. The Sand Creek Massacre proved to be the driving force needed to unite the Indian camps, including the Arkansas River and dog soldier bands; it was a union that ended decades of warring between the two.[54]

Bent watched for nearly a week as struggling survivors of his people entered the camp known as the "Bunch of Timbers." Black Kettle's wife had nine bullets in her but survived. Black Bear's wife had been struck with a bullet in her eye. After a long recovery, she was left so disfigured that she was forever known as One Eye Comes Together. During her recovery, she told others of the horror she had seen: the American soldiers had killed innocent children and raped women.

Bent estimated the dead to number 53 men and 110 women and children. However, Bent was unable to learn anything of his stepbrother Charley.

Meanwhile, as the anger over the slaughter of the Arapaho and Cheyenne people spread, several chiefs and warriors of the surrounding Indian societies gathered together for a war council. Black Kettle, as a respected member of the Cheyenne Council of Forty-Four, sat in during the war council. Several chiefs and pipe bearers left the camp to carry the war pipe to the Northern Arapaho on the Republican River and the Lakota on the Solomon River, as well as to the Sioux camps. George Bent and his brother-in-law, Edmond Guerrier, eagerly joined the pipe bearers on their journey to the other Indian camps. All agreed with the Cheyenne and smoked the war pipe. War had been declared. George Bent, along with his brother-in-law Ed Guerrier, another Sand Creek survivor, rode for the Purgatoire River in Colorado Territory and the home of George's father, William Bent. George wanted to inform his father of the impending war and learn news of any survivors, including his sisters, half brothers and stepmother.

With Bent's hip wound still healing, the trio rode slowly. Eventually, they reached the Arkansas River, just a few miles upriver from Fort Lyon. From a bluff above the river, Bent saw a large military camp. He could hear the soldiers singing, and straining to hear the melodies, he recognized Christmas carols. It was Christmas Eve. Bent decided to resume his travel after dark so as not to alert the soldiers. However, Guerrier, fearful of being caught by the soldiers, refused to go on. The only hope, as he saw it, was to surrender.

In the cover of darkness, Bent continued his journey alone. By midday, Bent arrived at the Bent ranch along the Purgatoire River. He arrived just in time for Christmas dinner. The Bent family reunion was an especially joyous one on this holy day of celebration. William Bent thought his son was dead. George was relieved to be greeted by Island, his stepmother, who he feared was dead. His older brother Robert was there, as was his sister Mary and her husband, Robison Moore; all were safe at the ranch.

George learned that his stepbrother Charley had been escorted to Fort Lyon by Captain Silas Soule. He was told that after being held prisoner for nearly a week, Charley was released and believed to be in one of the dog soldier camps at the "Big Timbers" area of the Smoky Hill River. George had news for the family as well. He reported that his sister Julia, married to Edmond Guerrier, was safe and in camp with the dog soldiers. He told his father of Guerrier's surrender but assured him he thought he was being treated fairly.

After George had spent nearly a week with his family, his hip wound was nearly healed. He knew it was time to return to Black Kettle's camp. In the last days of December 1864, George Bent left his father's ranch.

Arriving at the camp, it was the largest Indian village Bent had ever seen, nearly one thousand lodges strong. Settling into camp, Bent was present as

The South Platte River. *William Henry Jackson Jackson, 1867.*

the preparations were made for the raids along the Platte River, including a massive raid at the town of Julesburg, Colorado. The immediate concern was fortification of supplies. With Fort Rankin nearby, there would be an ample supply of goods, such as food, blankets, firearms and various necessities.

Fort Rankin was strategically located approximately one mile east of the settlement of Julesburg, near several fords of the South Platte River, where a branch of the Overland Trail, as well as the South Platte River Road, continued west.

Warriors from all the tribes readied for war, including the Cheyenne dog soldiers, of which both George and Charley Bent were now members. These warriors prepared their lances, shields, bows and arrows; only a few had firearms.

On January 7, 1865, Colorado Territory exploded with a rage of Indian revenge across the South Platte River Road. Several members of the dog soldiers split into smaller groups and conducted murderous raids along the river from Julesburg, west to American Ranch, a distance of over ninety miles.

It was an incredible attack, thoughtfully planned and brilliantly executed. The collective warriors, led by the Sioux, approached the bluff above Julesburg and hid in the sand hills. It was a crisp, cold night, yet it mattered not. Most of the warriors were deep in thought and preparation. A few hours before sunrise on January 7, 1865, the warriors prepared for the attack.

As the sun rose higher in the eastern sky, Big Crow, the chief of the Cheyenne Crooked Lance Society, led his warriors toward the fort. It was a deliberate ploy to bring the soldiers out of the fort. The ruse worked. The guards saw the Indians approaching and sounded the bugle alarm. The gates of the fort were thrown open, and over forty armed and mounted soldiers galloped out of the fort to confront the Indians. They were led in their charge by Captain O'Brien. Big Crow and his warriors then turned their horses and headed away from the fort, with the soldiers following in pursuit.

Amid the chase rode stage driver William M. Hudnut. He had arrived back at Julesburg station, where he received word that Indians were attacking in the area. Hudnut later testified:

> *Almost immediately, I saw the soldiers were retreating toward the station, the Indians in pursuit. Very soon, the detachment dashed past the station toward the fort, warning the people to save themselves if they could.*[55]

The Indians' decoy effort had worked perfectly, and the panic among the white settlers was an added benefit. George Bent recounted what happened next:

> *As soon as this was seen, the criers rode about camp, calling to the warriors to mount and get ready. Big Crow and his men retreated back toward the hills, drawing the soldiers after them. They came nearer and nearer, and it began to look like they would ride right into the trap; but as usual, the Indians would not wait for the right moment, and some young men suddenly broke away from the main force and charged out of the hills toward the soldiers. The rest of the thousand followed them, as there was no longer any use in hiding. The soldiers saw us swarming out of the hills and halted at once, then began to retreat. Big Crow and his party at once turned and charged the soldiers, being joined by a large body of Indians coming up from the rear. They struck the soldiers about three hundred yards from the stockade. In this first charge, Starving Elk killed the bugler, and several other soldiers fell. Some of the cavalrymen jumped off their horses to fight on foot but were at once surrounded; the rest of the troops, with their officer, galloped away toward the stockade, the Indians attacking them on all sides but not in strong enough force to cut them off and surround them. Some of these soldiers were killed, and all those who had dismounted also fell. Lieutenant [Eugene F.] Ware, who belonged to the Camp Rankin garrison but was not present during the fight, says that fourteen men were*

killed, one sergeant, three corporals, and ten privates. He gave all the names. I thought that more than this number fell, and a few weeks later, when the Indians attacked Julesburg again, I counted eighteen fresh graves near the stockade, but all these men may not have been killed in that fight.[56]

The Indians pounced on the soldiers, killing fifteen of the men, including a bugler, on whom many warriors first counted coup. Old Crow, mounted on a big bay horse, made the final attack on the bugler. Charging forward with both a tomahawk and a gun at the ready, he fired a bullet into the right cheek of the bugler. The bugler, with blood oozing from his mouth, fell off his horse.[57] He was later identified as nineteen-year-old Sergeant Alanson Hanchett.[58] The noted Cheyenne dog soldier Medicine Water took the bugler's horse as his prize. With the soldiers away in pursuit of the decoys, the remaining warriors were at their leave to plunder the area.

For the next few years, George Bent continued to ride with the Cheyenne dog soldiers to exact revenge on the white settlers. On January 26, 1865, a missive was sent from Fort Leavenworth to Colonel Moonlight with orders to burn the entire prairie south of the South Platte River from Kearny, Kansas Territory, west to Denver. This was in an effort to deter the Indians and their ruthless attacks on the innocent settlers. Army officers, positioned at different stations along the South Platte River Road, sent out detachments that set fire to the grasslands south of the river, some three hundred miles along the river. However, there seems to be much evidence that the burning did not have much of an effect, despite the winds—nor did it dissuade the Indians.

As George and his stepbrother Charley rode with and participated in raiding with the Cheyenne dog soldiers during this reign of terror along the South Platte River, he was not present during all the depredations.

On February 2, 1865, Bent was present during the second attack at Julesburg. The dog soldiers had cautiously approached the vicinity of the Julesburg Station and Camp Rankin. As the warriors descended on the unsuspecting settlement, they split their nearly one thousand warriors into three groups, nearly surrounding the area.

Lieutenant John Brewer, in temporary command of the military post, had less than fifty soldiers to defend the fort. They realized the futility of an attempt to defend the Julesburg settlement. As the Indian raid continued, Brewer managed to fire cannons from the fort in the direction of the approaching Indians. While it may have deterred the Indian attack at times, it did not stop the burning of Julesburg. The Indians took their time

Left: Cheyenne dog soldier Medicine Water led the attack on Julesburg. *Author's collection.*

Below: Cheyenne dog soldiers. *Library of Congress.*

burning the town. They set the buildings on fire one at a time, waiting for the structure to be fully engulfed in flame before torching the next one. This routine was repeated until every building in the small settlement was blazing, with plumes of smoke rising in the wind-blown prairie.

George Bent participated with the Cheyenne dog soldiers as they burned the town and taunted the soldiers at Camp Rankin.

> *When the village left the South Platte and started north a big war party, Sioux, Cheyennes, and Arapahos left the village and started down the river to finish up Julesburg. I went with the party, and again, the Indians tried the old trick of luring the soldiers out of their stockade by hiding the warriors among the hills and sending out a small party to tempt the soldiers out; but the troops this time were on their guard and would not stir outside their defenses, so after waiting among the sand hills for some time, our whole body charged out and raced across the flats to the stockade. The Indians circled around the stockade, yelling and shooting and taunting the soldiers to get them to come out and fight; but it was no use, so after a while, we withdrew east to the stage station. Here, the warriors, about six hundred strong, broke into the store and stage company warehouse and completely plundered both. In the hope of drawing the soldiers out, as soon as they had plundered the buildings, the Indians set fire to them, one by one, burning the stage station, telegraph office, store, warehouse, stables, etc., each separately. But no one came out. The great column of smoke floated up in the air, and it could be seen for twenty miles along the valley.*[59]

In the aftermath of the burning of the town and fort, George Bent headed west with a group of the Cheyenne dog soldiers. After traveling a few miles upriver of the South Platte River, Bent observed a company of soldiers riding east along the opposite side of the river. Evidently, they had noticed Bent as well, as suddenly, one of the officers rode toward the river bank, pulled his rifle and fired at Bent. Although the officer missed, Bent was enraged. He boldly rode alone to the water's edge and pulled his two pistols. Knowing he was out of range, he wildly fired the guns in the officer's direction, the bullets primarily landing on the ice of the frozen river. Bent was so angry that as he fired his pistols, he let loose a flurry of foul language directed toward the officer. With that, he calmly turned his horse around and rode back to his people.

By the spring of 1867, the Indian raids along the Arkansas and South Platte Rivers were causing great consternation for the federal government.

Colonel Jesse H. Leavenworth, an Indian agent for the Comanche and Kiowa tribes, was ordered by Commissioner of Indian Affairs Nathaniel G. Taylor to try to gather all the hostile tribes together for peace negotiations. Leavenworth had sent a message to George Bent, who was then living with the Cheyenne, camped along a stream in Texas known as "Bitter Water." The white settlers called it Sweet Water.

Leavenworth requested Bent's assistance in persuading as many of the chiefs as he could to attend the peace negotiations. Meanwhile, Leavenworth set about asking chiefs within his Indian agency to also attend.

George Bent was living in a lodge with his good friends Charlie Rath, a former employee of his father's at Bent's Fort, and Chief Santanta when he received the request from Fort Leavenworth for his help. Bent immediately set out to visit the various Indian camps and gain support from the chiefs.

During the many negotiations of what would become the Medicine Lodge Treaty of 1867, Black Kettle spoke for the Cheyenne. Major General William Selby Harney was so impressed that he presented Black Kettle with a fine horse.

George Bent was also well respected. He had proven himself to be a successful warrior among the Cheyenne dog soldiers. As the son of friend and trader William Bent and Owl Woman, the daughter of White Thunder, the keeper of the Cheyenne Sacred Medicine Arrows, Bent possessed some political clout within the tribe. Therefore, the marriage of George Bent and Magpie was advantageous for all concerned.

As such, the marriage ceremony was an extravagant affair. William Bent brought fourteen wagons loaded with trade goods as presents to the Cheyenne. Then Black Kettle presented his prized bay horse to the groom. Out of respect for his father, George had cut his hair and wore a black three-piece suit. However, he also wore finely beaded moccasins.

The bride was dressed in a long gown of deep blue trade cloth. Rows of elk teeth covered the top portion of her dress, and her skirt was quilled with intricate rows of beads in floral designs. Her jewelry consisted of silver rings and dangling silver earrings. Magpie also wore moccasins made of soft white antelope hides.[60]

Within a few months of his marriage, Bent returned to the dog soldiers, who continued to raid and war against their enemies. However, he did return to Black Kettle's camp long enough to be with Magpie when she gave birth to their first child, a girl whom Bent named Ada.

In April 1868, Bent returned to his father's home along the Purgatoire River. After a few days, Bent and his brother-in-law, Robison Moore, left for

George Bent married Magpie, Black Kettle's niece. *Denver Public Library.*

a tour of the area where Bent grew up and then stopped at Boggsville for a visit with Thomas Boggs and Christopher "Kit" Carson.

In the summer of 1868, Bent, Magpie and the baby were camped with Black Kettle's band when runners from Fort Larned sent word of soldiers moving in the region. Black Kettle had learned not to trust the soldiers. Before the day was over, the women had broken camp, and the band rode toward the Arkansas River crossing. There, Bent and his family, along with his brother-in-law Edmond Guerrier, parted with the rest of the band, heading southwest toward the Purgatoire River. Black Kettle led his people southeast toward the Washita River. It was the last time George Bent ever saw Black Kettle, the peaceful leader of the Cheyenne.

In January 1869, Bent took his family to Camp Supply, where he served as an interpreter for the newly created Indian agency for the Arapaho and Cheyenne. It was here that Magpie was reunited with her mother, Nis-ta-na. It was a joyful reunion, as they all thought Magpie had died at the battle of the Washita along with Black Kettle and many of his people. Magpie immediately took her mother into her lodge to live. However, according to Cheyenne custom, Bent was forbidden from making contact with or speaking to his mother-in-law. With tensions running high, Bent was soon banished from his lodge. He moved in with Kiowa Woman, an eighteen-year-old who had lost her parents at the Washita battle. A year later, Kiowa Woman bore Bent another daughter, whom he named Julia after his younger sister. For the next year, Bent operated a trading business at Camp Supply, where he could provide a living for his family. In 1870, Bent began working as an interpreter for Brinton Darlington, who wanted to provide free education to the children of the Arapaho and Cheyenne tribes. The Darlington Indian Agency was located on the north bank of the Canadian River in the Texas panhandle, very near Adobe Walls, the site of one of Bent's father's many forts.

In 1876, Bent moved his growing family to a reservation in Indian Territory. Bent, who by this time was a subchief, felt this was best, as his people were free to roam and hunt wild game on the reservation.

Bent lived in two lodges. One was with Kiowa Woman and their children, Julia and and George Jr. In the other lodge was Magpie, whom he had reconciled with some years previously. By this time, Magpie and Bent had had three more children, William and Mary, who both died in infancy, and Robert, who was born in 1872. In early 1879, Bent took a third wife. He had met twenty-one-year-old Standing Out Woman at the Darlington agency the previous year.

George Bent lived out his life on the Indian reservation located at El Reno, Oklahoma. Throughout the remainder of his life, George Bent would straddle life in two worlds. While living on the Indian reservation, he made strides in the education of the tribe's children. He became a Cheyenne historian, teaching the tribe's history and culture to new generations. At the same time, he worked with the government in procuring payment to the elders of the Cheyenne community, participated in local government and became the primary negotiator in land settlement issues.

In 1912, he began a lifelong correspondence with George Grinnell, who later published Bent's story. He also wrote many letters recounting his life to George Hyde, who would also publish Bent's life story in his own words. Historians have learned much of the Cheyenne way of life through these writings.

Possibly in an attempt to soften his own image, in one of his several letters to Hyde many years later, George Bent wrote the following regarding his years as a Cheyenne dog soldier:

> *The dog soldiers were "wild and reckless" and hard to control. However, they were excellent raiders and premier warriors, perpetually fomented by the failure* [to find] *food, the encircling encroachments of the white population, and the exasperating sense of decay and impending extinction with which they are surrounded.*

Sixty-three-year-old George Bent died on May 19, 1918, during the flu pandemic. He was buried in the Cheyenne custom, yet in the cemetery on the hill above town—a true testament to the man born into two worlds.

It would be nearly twenty years before his life story would finally be told.

FORT SEDGWICK

The fort, originally called Camp Rankin, was established on May 17, 1864, in the northeastern corner of Colorado Territory. It was strategically located approximately one mile east of the settlement of Julesburg. It was near several fords of the South Platte River, where a branch of the Overland Trail, as well as the South Platte River Road, continued westward. Brigadier General Robert B. Mitchell placed Colonel Christopher H. McNally of the Third U.S. Volunteer Regiment in command of the military post. Specifically built to provide protection for westward travelers, the fort also played a role in the Indian raids along the South Platte River Road. Nearly eighteen months after its construction, on September 27, 1865, Camp Rankin was designated Fort Sedgwick in honor of Major General John Sedgwick. Ironically, Sedgwick was killed at the Civil War Battle of Spotsylvania on May 9, 1865, a year before Camp Rankin was established. Jules Beni, a French trader, established the town of Julesburg in 1859 as a trading post along the South Platte River. From the beginning, this was an important stop along the Overland Trail, as the trail split in two different directions at this point. The north trail followed the Platte River through Wyoming and South Pass, on to California and Oregon. The southern trail followed the South Platte River to the early settlement of Denver City and on to Utah.

George Bent later described the fort and Julesburg:

> In 1865, Julesburg was an important place on the stage line; here, the company had a large station house…with an eating house, a big stable,

Left: Major John Sedgwick. *Library of Congress.*

Below: Fort Sedgwick. *Public domain.*

Opposite: Fort Sedgwick. *Anton Schonborn, 1870.*

blacksmith and repair shop, granary, and storehouses, and a big corral enclosed by a high wall built of sod. Besides the stage company's property, there was a large store selling all kinds of goods to travelers and emigrant trains, and the Overland Telegraph Company also had an office at this point. Altogether, Julesburg Station was quite a large place for the plains in those days. The buildings here were partly built of cottonwood logs and partly of sod.[61]

Following the brutal massacre of innocent Cheyenne and Arapaho Indians at Sand Creek, on November 29, 1864, the Plains Indians formed an alliance of war and revenge, the likes of which the western settlers had

never experienced. Indian war councils were held in whcih the peace pipe was smoked among many tribes that had been at war against one another for over forty years. The conclusion among all was war against the white man. John L. Sipes, a Cheyenne Nation historian, wrote:

> *The tradition of the war pipe, when necessary, was sent out in the spring, but after the slaughter at Sand Creek, the war pipe went out in the winter, this was early December. To my knowledge, from the old ones, never before had the war pipe been sent in the time of winter until after Sand Creek.*

As preparations for raids along the Platte River were made, the immediate concern was fortification of supplies, as the survivors had nothing. Following several small raids along the Platte River, the warriors set their sights on Camp Rankin, as the military post would have an ample supply of goods to replace the loss they suffered at the massacre in food, blankets and various necessities. Meanwhile, shortly after sunrise on January 6, 1868, William M. Hudnut, a driver for the Holladay Overland Mail Express Company, operating in conjunction with the famed Pony Express operation, arrived at the Julesburg station. They had been chased for four miles by members of the Cheyenne dog soldiers. After receiving fresh horses, Hudnut drove on to Camp Rankin, one mile away. Hudnut immediately sought an audience with Captain Nicholas

Julesburg depot. *Public domain, 1886.*

J. O'Brien of the Seventh Iowa Cavalry, Company F, who was temporarily stationed at Camp Rankin. Hudnut asked O'Brien to provide a military escort for his stage so that he could arrive safely in Denver. O'Brien refused, stating that he had a small force and that they were needed to defend the fort and nearby citizens. An argument ensued, and a defiant O'Brien finally dismissed Hudnut by stating he believed the danger of traveling was greatly exaggerated. O'Brien was about to find out how wrong he was.

On a crisp, cold night in January 1865, the collective warriors, over one thousand, including Cheyenne, Sioux and Arapaho, led by the Cheyenne dog soldiers, approached the bluff above Julesburg. There, they spent the night in the sand hills, preparing for the attack. Many of the warriors applied war paint, while others gathered together their lances, shields, bows and arrows. There were only a few firearms among the men.

At dawn on January 7, 1865, one group of warriors, led by Big Crow, quietly approached the fort and rushed the guards outside the fort walls. The soldiers returned fire, and then the gates of the fort opened, with over forty mounted soldiers in pursuit of the Indian war party. It was an incredible attack, thoughtfully planned and executed brilliantly. The decoy strategy worked perfectly. The Indian scouts sent the signal, and the hidden warriors converged upon the fort and nearby sutler quarters. They rushed forward with bloodcurdling yells of vengeance. Several years later, Captain Nicholas

J. O'Brien recalled the incident and described the Indian yells for a *Rocky Mountain News* reporter:

> *The first warning was the weird yelling….As we advanced forward, the Indians retreated toward an arroya known as Devil's Dive, a well-known point of ambush.*[62]

With the soldiers away in pursuit of the decoys, the remaining warriors were free to plunder the area of the fortress. Barrels of flour, sugar and molasses were taken, as well as sacks of cornmeal, beans, sides of bacon and canned goods. Both George and Charles Bent, members of the Cheyenne dog soldiers and the half-Indian sons of the famed fort owner William Bent, participated in the raid. George Bent later recalled the plundering, saying the Indians did not understand things in a can and were disgusted when George opened a can of oysters and slurped down the contents.

Bent also recounted the discovery of green paper by the Indians. Not knowing it was federal currency, they threw it aside, at which point, Bent, who knew all too well the value of the money, scurried to scoop it up. Bent also found a new soldier's uniform, which he took and proudly wore in future Indian raids.

Included in this war party were the many women who traveled with the group, and they herded the extra horses needed to carry the supplies obtained back to their camp. Among these women was Mo-chi, a survivor of Sand Creek who insisted on helping her people in whatever way she could. When the warriors were observed leaving the fort, Mo-chi and the other women led the packhorses and began loading the goods onto them. As the warriors began leaving the scene, Mo-chi busied herself with herding the captured horses. Meanwhile, the pursuing soldiers who had followed the decoys, amazingly, and perhaps in confusion, had dismounted and staged a counter-fight. The warriors pounced on the soldiers, killing fifteen, including a bugler, whom many warriors first counted coup on. When Old Crow made the final attack of death, Cheyenne warrior Medicine Water took the reins of the bugler's horse as his prize. The victorious warriors made their way to the retreating group, where Medicine Water turned his prize horse loose with Mo-chi's herd.[63]

The Indians retreated from the fort and the Julesburg area for a time, as the U.S. Army quickly responded. Within thirty days of the attack, the U.S. Army sent additional troops to guard stage stops and various trails, including the Overland Trail and the South Platte River Road.

The burning of Julesburg. *Public domain, 1865.*

The Indians responded by simply changing tactics and destinations; the raids continued. On February 18, 1868, the Indians returned. This time, the town of Julesburg was raided and burned to the ground. In a panic, the citizens ran the mile to Camp Rankin and watched as their town burned. As the military garrison did not have enough troops on hand to defend the town, the few soldiers there also watched the carnage. In the end, eighteen citizens were killed.

The town relocated two miles north of the army post. The town of Julesburg would move two more times, unprecedented in Colorado history.

When Camp Rankin was renamed Fort Sedgwick in September 27, 1865, it was enlarged and fortified with additional military troops, including the Seventh Iowa Cavalry. For the next six years, the soldiers at Fort Sedgwick held to a strict policy of holding all westward travelers and wagon trains at the fort until officers were able to ascertain no sign of hostile Indians and deem the road safe for travel. In 1867, when the Union Pacific Railroad built rails west from Nebraska, troops from Fort Sedgwick were assigned to protect the construction workers from the threat of Indian attacks.

On May 31, 1871, Fort Sedgwick was officially closed by the U.S. Army. Years later, its flagpole was moved to the town of Julesburg, where it is now on display in front of the library. Today, a stone marker sits at the site of the fort. Nearby is the cemetery where several soldiers are buried.[64]

WILLIAM FREDERICK "BUFFALO BILL" CODY

FRONTIER SHOWMAN

William Frederick Cody was born on February 26, 1846, just west of Mississippi River, near LeClaire, Iowa. As a child of the West, Cody would one day become the epitome of the frontier West. In 1852, Isaac Cody moved his family to Leavenworth, Kansas. Cody loved the open prairie, where he could ride his prized horse Prince, a gift from his father. In 1857, after an illness, Cody's father, Isaac, died. Cody later wrote:

> *This sad event left my mother and the family in poor circumstances, and I determined to follow the plains for a livelihood for them and myself.*

At the age of eleven, Cody went to work as a wagon driver for the freighting company of Russell, Major and Waddell, based in Leavenworth. The company carried loads from Leavenworth to Salt Lake City. Cody later wrote, "The country was alive with buffalos," and the eleven-year-old participated in his first buffalo hunt in 1857. It was also in 1857 that Cody said he first met famed gunman Wild Bill Hickok. According to Cody, Hickok stopped another teamster from bullying him.

> *From that time forward, Wild Bill was my protector and intimate friend, and the friendship thus begun continued until his death.*[65]

The following year, Cody headed for the Colorado Rockies during the Pikes Peak gold rush of 1858–59. When that didn't pan out, Cody returned to freighting and even spent some time at a school in Leavenworth, Kansas. However, he soon became bored. Cody wrote:

> *I longed for the cool air of the mountains; and to the mountains, I determined to go.*

William F. Cody as a young Indian scout. *Denver Public Library.*

While in Leavenworth, Cody saw an advertisement for young riders for the newly created Pony Express. At the age of fourteen, the wiry teenager easily qualified for the advertised position—"skinny, expert riders willing to risk death daily." Cody was one of eighty young men hired by the firm of Russell, Majors and Waddell to ride for the Pony Express. Cody worked as a messenger at the Julesburg station under Jack Slade. His route was a forty-five-mile run between Red Buttes and Three Crossings. The famed Pony Express was in operation for a short eighteen months before it was replaced by the telegraph.

Despite Pony Express owner Alexander Majors's claim that Cody was indeed an employee, some historians are doubtful. Steve Friesen, the former director of the Buffalo Bill Museum and Grave Site on Lookout Mountain, Colorado, and the latest biographer of Cody, offers this perspective regarding Cody's participation the historic event:

> *Those who question Cody's involvement with the Pony Express have suggested he invented his association with it to add to his reputation. One could ask, "Did William F. Cody become famous because of the Pony Express or did the Pony Express become famous because of William F. Cody?"* Were it not for the recreation of a Pony Express ride in Buffalo Bill's Wild West *for nearly thirty years, it might have ended up as a minor footnote in American history.*[66]

During the summer of 1862, Cody worked as a guide for military troops during the Civil War. Two years later, he officially enlisted with the war effort. On February 19, 1864, eighteen-year-old Cody signed on with the Seventh Kansas Volunteer Cavalry. Following the end of the war, Cody was mustered out of service on September 29, 1865. Cody maintained a strong relationship with the military, although in a civilian capacity.

A few months later, Cody moved to Saint Louis, Missouri, were Louisa Frederici lived. He had met her in the city during his service in the Civil War. On March 6, 1866, twenty-one-year-old William Frederick Cody and twenty-four-year-old Louisa Maud Frederici were married. The newlyweds moved to Cody's hometown of Leavenworth. However, within a few months, Cody asked to again scout for the army.

In 1867, Cody was hired by the Kansas Pacific Railroad to hunt for meat for the workers as the railroad company built tracks westward. With his trusted horse Brigham and his favorite hunting rifle, an 1866 Springfield that he named "Lucretia Borgia," Cody proved to be quite effective at his new job. He later wrote:

> As soon as one buffalo would fall, Brigham would take me so close to the next that I could almost touch it with my gun.

The railroad workers were so impressed that they began calling Cody "Buffalo Bill," and the name stuck with him for the rest of his illustrious life. When his work was completed for the railroad, Cody returned to scouting for the army. He worked with great generals of the day, such as Eugene A. Carr and Philip H. Sheridan. For ten years, from the age of eleven to the age of twenty-one, Cody was a part of more western adventures than many frontiersmen experienced in a lifetime. But he was just getting started.

During the Indian wars in the latter part of the 1860s and into the 1870s, Cody worked as a contract employee for the army. In the spring of 1869, the Cheyenne dog soldiers, led by Tall Bull, were raiding settlers' homes, burning buildings and taking hostages. General Philip Sheridan put together a force of army troops to launch a campaign against the raiding Indian party and rescue the captives. Major General Eugene A. Carr was selected to lead this campaign. Sheridan suggested that Carr enlist the scouting services of Cody. In Sheridan's written recommendation, he cited Cody's service during the previous year, including a particular incident in which Cody rode horseback over three hundred miles in under sixty hours. Sheridan wrote:

> Such an exhibition of endurance and courage was more than enough to convince me that his services would be extremely valuable in the [upcoming] campaign, so I retained him at Fort Hays till the battalion of the Fifth Cavalry arrived and then made him chief of scouts for that regiment.[67]

At a spot known as Elephant Rock, Major General Carr ordered his regiments of the Fifth Cavalry into battle on May 13, 1869. Carr and his men were successful, defeating the warriors handily. Twenty-five warriors were dead, while Carr lost only four soldiers. Three days later, Carr's men again attacked the Cheyenne group and were victorious. Again, Cody proved his skills as a scout, prompting Major General Carr to write:

Our scout William Cody, who has been with the detachment since last September, displayed great skill in following it [the trail] *and also deserves great credit for his fighting in both engagements, his marksmanship being very conspicuous. He deserves honorable mention for this and other services, and I hope to be able to retain him as long as I am engaged in this duty.*[68]

Cody was injured during this fight when a bullet cut an inch-long gap in his scalp. Obviously in pain and bleeding profusely, Cody nevertheless volunteered to ride through the night the fifty miles to Fort Kearny for reinforcements. Cody would remain with Carr's regiment and again prove his scouting and fighting abilities.

General Carr and his Fifth Cavalry were in the area of the Republican River Valley. Led by Cody, the troops had been scouting for the Indian trails since the engagement with Tall Bull and the Cheyenne dog soldiers the previous month. On June 20, 1869, General C.C. Augur sent a message via courier in the field to General Carr, notifying him of a Cheyenne raid along the Saline River in Kansas, where female settlers, including Susanna Alderdice, had been captured by members of Tall Bull's dog soldiers. General John Schofield, the commander of the U.S. Department of the Missouri, sent a missive requesting that "such efforts as may be practable [*sic*] be made by the troops in his [Carr's] department to rescue these captives."

Not only was this a military expedition, but it had now become a rescue mission. Carr's Fifth Cavalry, with Cody as chief scout, was reinforced with a company of Pawnee scouts under the command of Major Frank Joshua North, as well as a subordinate officer, his brother Captain Luther H. North. Carr's troops totaled nearly five hundred.

On June 28, Carr and his men reached the Republican River, which they followed west. Along the way, with Carr in the lead, he discovered the Indian trail. Carr later described the incident:

I dismounted the command so as not to hurt the tracks and sent for "Buffalo Bill," who was hunting antelopes off to the right, and told him to look at that! He said, "By Gee Hosaphat, that is the trail!" And I felt quite cocky at being the first to find it. It had drawn close together to make as little show as possible when it had to cross the river and went into the bluffs on the north side. It then went parallel with the line of the valley to the westward, crossing the ridges and ravines, keeping five or ten miles away from the river bottom and camping on hidden springs, which the Indians knew.[69]

Carr and Cody both concurred that the lodge pole trails they found were not over a week old. The trail also revealed tracks made by shod animals. As the soldiers followed the river southwest in Nebraska Territory, Carr divided his command. On July 2, 1869, Carr and his troops, while camped on the south fork of the Republican River, had a skirmish with a group of dog soldiers.

On July 9, Carr and his troops, as well as the scouts, made their way some thirty miles into Colorado Territory. Following the Indian trail, Cody and Major Frank North discovered a woman's shoeprint in the dirt that was distinctly different from a moccasin print. The soldiers pushed on. The following day, Cody easily picked up the trail of Tall Bull and his Cheyenne dog soldiers. Cody led Carr's troops to an area known as Summit Springs, located between the Republican and South Platte Rivers in today's Logan County.

Before sunrise on Sunday, July 11, 1869, Cody led Carr and his soldiers to a ridge overlooking the South Platte River, where the Cheyenne camp could be seen in the distance. There, Carr took some time to rest the weary horses and gather the military force into formation for an attack on the Indian village. Carr ordered his troops into two columns, each ready to charge the Indian camp from separate directions. Against a howling prairie wind, the soldiers charged from the northeast toward the Indian camp. The soldiers were quickly able to overtake the village. Panic and pandemonium caused the people of the Indian village to run out of their lodges, only to be shot down before they knew what was happening. Those who were able to escape went south of the village as the soldiers continued their onslaught of fire.

Carr later reported that one soldier was wounded, and he estimated the Indian dead to number between fifty and seventy-five. He also reported that there were over eighty tipis in the camp. However, a group of the dog soldiers, including Tall Bull, had gathered at the southeast area of the Indian camp. Here, they wielded their lances, shields and clubs, as well as what few firearms they possessed, in a brave but futile attempt to fight the soldiers. In the ensuing battle, Tall Bull was killed. George Bent, a half-

Indian man who rode with the dog soldiers, recounted the death of Tall Bull as related to him by Two Crows:

> *Tall Bull, the dog soldier chief, had three wives. One of those he put on a horse when the shooting started, and she got away with a daughter of the first wife. The other two wives, the youngest and the eldest, went with Tall Bull to the ravine. The Cheyennes in the ravine put up a desperate fight. Bill Cody and Frank North claim they killed Tall Bull, but the Pawnees say no one knows who killed him, as they were all shooting at him.*[70]

Nevertheless, years later, when Cody launched his worldwide famous *Wild West Show*, he included a reenactment of the Battle of Summit Springs, with himself as the killer of Tall Bull. This led to decades of controversy over who actually killed Tall Bull on July 11, 1869. Just two weeks after the Battle of Summit Springs, while at Fort McPherson, Nebraska, Cody met the infamous dime novelist Ned Buntline. Perhaps already thinking of elevating his frontier celebrity status, on July 24, 1869, Cody allowed Buntline to accompany him on a scouting expedition. Following the adventure, Buntline wrote the first of many stories about the now famous scout. "Buffalo Bill: The King of the Border Men" was a serial story published in the *New York Weekly*.

Back at Fort McPherson, Cody was joined by his wife, Louisa, and their three-year-old daughter, Arta Lucille. Here, their second child, Kit Carson Cody, was born in the summer of 1870. With Cody's scouting services in high demand, the Cody family would remain at the fort for the next few years.

Military leaders who visited the fort, including General Philip Sheridan, often requested a hunting trip with Cody. In the winter of 1872, Cody learned that the Russian Grand Duke Alexei, while visiting America, desired a buffalo hunt with Cody. True to form, Cody scouted the area around the fort in an effort to find a region where buffalo were plentiful. When the duke arrived at Fort McPherson for his buffalo hunt, Cody graciously offered his army-issued horse Buckskin Joe for the grand duke to ride. Also accompanying Cody was his friend and scouting partner Texas Jack Omohundro. After several attempts at shooting his prey with a revolver, Cody loaned the grand duke his prized rifle "Lucretia Borgia." Within a matter of minutes, the Russian dignitary brought down his first buffalo. During the hunt, which lasted several days, the grand duke was able to kill many buffalo. News reporters who were invited to cover the event all wrote glowing reports of "Buffalo Bill."

The death of Tall Bull, as reenacted by Buffalo Bill. *From Frank Winch,* Thrilling Lives of Buffalo Bill and Pawnee Bill, *first hardcover edition (New York: S.L. Parsons, 1911).*

With such popularity, Cody was invited to New York. Several men Cody had taken on hunting trips treated him to a lavish party in his honor. This was followed by several social engagements. Cody later wrote:

> *I received numerous dinner invitations, as well as invitations to visit different places of amusement and interest; but as they came in so thick and fast, I soon became badly demoralized and confused.*

While still in New York, on February 20, 1872, Cody attended the opening night of a new play at the Bowery Theatre on the lower east side of Manhattan. Ned Buntline's *New York Weekly* story "Buffalo Bill: The King of the Border Men" was the subject of the play. Cody wrote:

> *I was curious to see how I would look when represented by someone else, and of course, I was present on opening night, a private box having been reserved for me.*

Evidently, from this experience, the celebrity limelight took hold of Cody. With the encouragement of Ned Buntline, Cody staged his own play in New York City. Cody wrote:

> *It was time to try my luck behind the footlights. My new drama was arranged for the stage by J. V. Arlington, the actor. It was a five-act play, without head or tail, and it made no difference at which act we commenced the performance.*

Written by Ned Buntline, the play, titled *Scouts of the Prairie*, included his longtime friends and fellow scouts Wild Bill Hickok and Texas Jack Omohundro. Not surprising, Buntline wrote in an additional character, which he played himself. The play opened on December 16, 1872, in Chicago, Illinois. The play was an instant success and played in various venues across America. However, after two years, Hickok left the production. It was the last time Cody would see his old friend.

For the American centennial celebration in 1876, Cody launched his new play *Life on the Border*, which recreated the nation's past and future. It was during this time that Cody penned his own largely fictional dime novels, including *Death Trailer, the Chief of Scouts*. These publications added to his already enormous popularity.

Just as New York City's 1876 theatrical season was in full swing, Cody learned that his five-year-old son, Kit, had contracted scarlet fever and was near death. Cody took the train to his home in Rochester, where his family resided. Both Cody and Louisa were at Kit's bedside when he died on April 22, 1876.

It was shortly after this sad event that Cody learned of the Indian conflict in the Black Hills. Cody suspended his then-current production, telling his audience that he was riding off to join the Indian Wars of the Plains. On June 10, 1876, Cody was accepted into the Fifth Cavalry as the chief of scouts. Barely into his new assignment, Cody, along with the rest of his fellow soldiers, learned of the defeat of the Seventh Cavalry, led by George Armstrong Custer at the Battle at the Little Big Horn in Southern Montana. Cody had once scouted for the general and was sad to hear of his death. Nearly the entire Seventh Cavalry was killed in the battle. Most of the country learned of Custer's defeat at the opening of the Centennial Fair on July 4, 1876.

On July 17, 1876, Cody guided a a battalion of the Fifth Calvary, under the command of Colonel Wesley Merritt, to an area along War Bonnet

Creek in Nebraska. There, the soldiers engaged in a skirmish with Cheyenne warriors. When Cody spotted Yellow Hair, a Cheyenne subchief, he leveled his Winchester carbine at him and killed him. Christian Madsen, an eyewitness, later wrote that Cody then pulled out his Bowie knife and scalped the warrior. Waving the bloody scalp in the air, Cody shouted, "The first scalp for Custer!"[71] Seeing their leader killed and the force of the military, the remainder of the war party quickly fled. Before the soldiers left the area, Cody retrieved Yellow Hair's war bonnet and his weapons. He would later send them, as well as the scalp, to his Rochester home.

Two weeks later, Cody received word of the death of his friend Wild Bill Hickok. On August 2, 1876, Hickok had been murdered by a gunshot to the back of the head in a saloon in Deadwood, South Dakota. Cody wrote:

> *Thus ended the career of a lifelong friend of mine who, in spite of his many faults, was a noble man, ever brave and generous-hearted.*

Cody remained with the Fifth Calvary until September 1876, when he resigned his commission and returned to Rochester. Within a month, Cody, ever the showman, returned to the stage with a new play, *Red Right Hand; or Buffalo Bill's First Scalp for Custer*. For the next year, Cody toured the country and regaled his audiences with a melodramatic reenactment of killing and scalping of Yellow Hair, complete with the actual scalp.

When the play ended in the fall of 1877, Cody joined his scouting colleague Frank North on a personal scouting expedition. The two traveled to Nebraska in search of suitable land for a cattle ranch. They found it near North Platte, Nebraska. Cody toured for another year and then moved his family to the new ranch. Of the move to the West, which was permanent, Cody wrote:

> *I was leaving a comfortable little home, where I was sure of making a good living for my family; while, on the other hand, I was embarking on a sea of uncertainty.*

Cody thoroughly enjoyed the freedom he felt on the plains while roaming his cattle ranch in the saddle. It was during these solitary moments that Cody formulated his idea of an extravagant show featuring aspects of the Wild West he saw slipping away every day. For the next two years, Cody presented new plays in various venues across the country, all the while incorporating acts that he would later expand in his Wild West extravaganza.

Buffalo Bill's Wild West and Congress of Rough Riders of the World. Buffalo: Courier Litho Co., circa 1899; Library of Congress.

Cody called on his many friends and colleagues to participate in his new entertainment venture. And they did not disappoint. Many provided animals, including buffalo, horses and burros.

Some of the Indians Cody had befriended over the years, such as the Pawnee and Lakota, also signed on. Others provided myriad props, including a stagecoach and Conestoga wagon. Cody's friend Frank North joined the effort, as did a scout from Oklahoma, Gordon Lillie, also known as Pawnee Bill. Cody also included thirteen-year-old Johnny Baker, a kid he had befriended in North Platte.

Rehearsals for Cody's outdoor show were held at the local fairgrounds in Columbus, Nebraska. Finally, when costumes such as buckskin and rodeo apparel arrived, Cody sold his show to venues across the West. The grand opening occurred on May 17, 1883, in Omaha, Nebraska. There were two performances that day, with an audience of ten thousand at the first and an astonishing twenty thousand at the second performance. The *Bloomington Bulletin* of May 24, 1883, reported the event, writing, in part:

> *The audience cheered at trifles and blazed with enthusiasm at any demonstration of merit. The picture was an extraordinary one, such as we are not likely to see again.*

The reporter could not not have been more mistaken. *Buffalo Bill's Wild West Show* would have an amazing run of over three decades. Interestingly enough—and most likely by design—Cody was not billed to perform during the opening show. However, when the audience began chanting "Buffalo Bill! Buffalo Bill!" Cody grabbed his nickel-plated .44-caliber 1873 Winchester and from the sidelines, mounted his horse and galloped out to the center of the arena. There, a series of glass balls were thrown into the air, which Cody, in true showman form, promptly shot. Cody's marksmanship would remain a favorite act in the show.[72]

The opening of the 1884 season occurred in Saint Louis, Missouri, with tours throughout the East, including a stop in Elmira, New York. In the audience was Mark Twain, who wrote a letter to Cody, dated September 10, 1884:

> *I have now seen your* Wild West Show *two days in succession and have enjoyed it thoroughly. It brought back vividly the breezy, wild life of the great plains and the Rocky Mountains and stirred me like a war song. Down to its smallest details, the show is genuine—cowboys, vaqueros, Indians, stagecoach, costumes and all; it is wholly free from sham and insincerity, and the effects produced upon me by its spectacles were identical with those wrought upon me a long time ago by the same spectacles on the frontier.*

Following the final performance of the 1885 season in New Orleans, Cody was introduced to a female markswoman with some notoriety, Phoebe Ann Moses, who was known by her stage name, Annie Oakley. After an impressive demonstration, Cody hired the twenty-five-year-old Oakley as the featured attraction in the sharpshooter portion of the show.

With the opening of the 1886 season, Cody had another featured attraction, Lakota chief Sitting Bull. The legendary Indian leader was presented to the audience as he resolutely rode his horse around the arena. Sitting Bull very much enjoyed watching the marksmanship of Annie Oakley and called her "Little Sure Shot." Sitting Bull did not return for a second season with the *Wild West Show*. In an interview with the *New York Tribune Weekly*, dated November 26, 1886, Cody was quoted regarding his impression of Sitting Bull:

> *In war,* [Sitting Bull] *was a bitter opponent, in peace, he won my friendship and sympathy; he impressed me as a deep thinker, conscientious as to the proper rights to the lands of their fathers.*

Cody began planning for his biggest *Wild West Show* ever. He had long thought of taking the show to Europe, and with the 1887 season, he made it a reality. It was an enormous undertaking. On March 31, 1887, Buffalo Bill Cody, along with Annie Oakley, Cody's foster son Johnny Baker and several Native Americans, all boarded the *State of Nebraska* steamship in New York Harbor, bound for England. Stowed in the cargo area were dozens of crates containing props and costumes, as well as several animals. Cody had timed his opening show in Europe to coincide with Britain's Golden Jubilee celebration.

Cody's *Wild West Show* predictably played to sell-out crowds, as Europe had never seen anything like it before. It was an outdoor performance of huge proportions, and Cody did not disappoint. And European high society did not disappoint Cody. Cody was invited to dinners hosted by the influential Churchill family, and he was invited to another with the Prince of Wales. Cody had tea with Oscar Wilde and was a special guest before Parliament.

During the five months *Buffalo Bill's Wild West Show* performed in London, there were special performances at Earl's Court for dignitaries, including the Prince of Wales and Queen Victoria. When the queen saluted the American flag, it was the first time in history that such an act of respect had been demonstrated by a member of England's royalty. Cody later wrote:

> *I am convinced—and I say it in no boastful spirit—that our visit to England has set the population of the British Islands reading, thinking and talking about their American kinsman to an extent before unprecedented.*

In the final tour of the show in Manchester, Cody invited various dignitaries to dine with him on a feast of American fare, including fried chicken, Boston baked beans, corn cakes and pie. Known as Fourth of July dinners, they would become a traditional part of Cody's farewell performances when performing overseas. In the spring of 1889, Cody brought his *Wild West Show* back to Europe, performing in France, Spain and Italy. Opening in Paris with French president Marie François Sadi Carnot in attendance, the show played to a packed audience. For the next six months, *Buffalo Bill's Wild West Show* played two shows daily. While in Italy, the entourage performed in the historic Roman Colosseum ruins. It was during this European tour that cowboy hats were in high demand. This sparked a marketing idea by Cody, and future European tours included several American West items for sale at the shows.

Cody capitalized on a great opportunity to bring his show to thousands of Americans at the 1893 World's Colombian Exposition held in Chicago,

Illinois. When Cody was told he could not perform inside the confines of the exposition, he simply acquired land across from the entrance and set up his *Wild West Show*. There, *Buffalo Bill's Wild West Show* played to audiences as large as eighteen thousand for a full month before the exposition opened on May 1, 1893.

After the Chicago shows, Cody finally returned to his home near North Platte, Nebraska. It had been years since he had been home, and the town welcomed its celebrity with a parade complete with a brass band. When Cody noticed the band was not in uniform, he promptly purchased uniforms for all the band members. Cody, known to be a generous benefactor, provided the needed funds for a housing project in North Platte in 1911.

For the next several years, Cody remained, for the most part, at his Nebraska ranch. Now a very wealthy man, Cody invested in several business opportunities in an effort to increase his wealth. In 1894, the arrival of the Chicago, Burlington and Quincy Railroad in the small town of Sheridan, Wyoming, just south of the site of the Battle of the Little Big Horn, piqued Cody's interest. Cody's oldest daughter, Arta, and her husband, Horton Boal, lived in Sheridan. Cody formed the W.F. Cody Hotel Company, which eventually became instrumental in constructing the Sheridan Inn, the largest hotel in town.[73]

The following year, Cody set his sights on founding a town west of Sheridan in the Bighorn Basin of Wyoming. A section of land was purchased, and a town appropriately named Cody was platted. For the next decade, Cody would return to the area, purchasing land and ranches, including the TE Ranch. He would also utilize his hotel company in the building of the Irma Hotel, named in honor of his youngest daughter. Later, Cody would build a hunting lodge just outside of Yellowstone. He called the lodge the Pahaska Tepee, which was his Lakota given name, meaning "long hair." Although Cody spent time and money developing his namesake town, he was disappointed that it never really grew—that is, during his lifetime.

In 1910, William F. Cody, now sixty-four years old, decided it was time to retire from the beloved entertainment stage he had created. Perhaps Cody's biographer, Steve Friesen, put it best when he wrote:

> *Cody wanted to help forge the New West, but it was the Wild West that was his greatest success.*[74]

Cody, along with his partner Gordon Lillie, who used the stage name "Pawnee Bill," launched a two-year farewell tour across America. The headliner of the show was Johnny Baker, Cody's foster son. Under the show name "Cowboy Kid," Baker displayed his expert marksmanship. Baker also became the show manager for this farewell tour. Baker had filled many roles over the years, and Cody was extremely grateful to him, as this letter, dated November 12, 1908, clearly states:

> *Dear Johnnie, I cannot express my feelings to you in words, for you are so near and dear to my heart. For twenty-three years, you have never once failed me. No father ever had a son more loving and faithful. You have done so much to make* Buffalo Bill's Wild West *what it is, as I have myself. You have been with it from its conception and filled nearly every capacity in it. I would not be able to go on with it now without you.*[75]

In a strange twist of fate, the newly formed Showman's League of America had asked Cody to serve as the first president. It came, ironically enough, when attendance at his shows was dropping at a steady rate. Nevertheless, Cody received a loan from Harry H. Tammen, the owner and publisher of the *Denver Post*, to continue his *Wild West Show* for another season. The $20,000 loan, at 6 percent interest, was due in six months. Cody learned, too late, that Tammen's generosity was not what it seemed. He knew Cody would be unable to repay the loan and intended to merge the *Wild West Show* with his own Sells-Floto Circus. Tammen felt it would be a sure way to knock out the competition: the Ringling Bros. Circus.[76]

Tammen wasted no time announcing the merger in the February 5, 1913 issue of the *Denver Post*:

> *The most important deal ever consummated in American amusement enterprise was closed in Denver a few days ago, when Colonel W.F. Cody (Buffalo Bill) put his name to a contract with the proprietors of the Sells-Floto Circus, the gist of which is that these two big shows consolidate for the season of 1914 and thereafter. This circus is now in its twelfth year. Everyone remembers the fights with the Ringling Brothers, Barnam and Bailey Circus and other attractions which combined in what is commonly known as "the circus trust." The present combination would seem to make Sells-Floto shows the monarchs of the amusement field.*

Tammen and his partner Frederick Gilmer Bonfils got the selling attraction they needed: Colonel William F. "Buffalo Bill" Cody. As Tammen predicted, when the six-month loan came due, Cody could not repay. When the final show on July 21 ended, the Denver Sheriff's Department shut down the show and seized its property. A month later, an auction was held at Overland Park. The *Denver Post* covered the event in its August 27, 1913 issue. Under the headline "Half of *Wild West Show* Sold at Auction for High Prices," the reporter wrote:

> *The bidding was fast. To the man who doesn't know what a thousand dollars looks like, it seemed that the men out there cared no more for a hundred dollar bill than a hog does for Sunday.*

Several of Cody's friends were present at the auction. When Cody's favorite horse, Isham, was presented, Cody's friends participated in the bidding process. Finally, the gavel came down on a $150 bid. Cody's old friend Colonel C.J. Bills led the horse to the sidelines, where Cody stood, and handed the reins to Cody.

Cody was contractually obligated to perform with the Sells-Floto Circus. Cody was the only attraction amid the circus's parade of animals and clown tricks. Cody hated it, and after the 1915 season, he quit. Cody spent the rest of that year working on his autobiography and marketing several moving pictures he had made. W.R. Hearst agreed to print portions of Cody's writings in a series published in Hearst's *International* magazine.

In 1916, Cody, now seventy years old, agreed to join the *Miller and Arlington Wild West Show*, affiliated with the Miller brothers' famous 101 Ranch in Oklahoma. Cody enjoyed touring with this show, which included elements of his own, including marksmanship, rather than the circus he had been forced to work with. Both Cody and Johnny Baker performed for the audience, although Cody no longer rode a horse.

Following the close of the show on November 11, 1916, Cody went to his sister Mary Decker's house in Denver. May, as she was known, cared for her brother for the next two weeks. Finally, when his health seemed much improved, Cody left for a series of western visits. However, in mid-December, Cody arrived by train back in Denver. Alarmed by her brother's condition, May sent for Doctor J.P. East and then wired Louisa in Nebraska. Dr. East diagnosed Cody's condition as uremic poisoning. There was nothing he could do. To ease Cody's pain and offer him some relief, East accompanied him on a trip to the hot springs at Glenwood Springs. Cody improved somewhat, but it was temporary.

Back in Denver, members of the immediate family held vigil at May Decker's house. Cody's grandson and namesake, Cody Boel, later wrote:

We played games of high five, and I remember when I played as his partner, his opponents sluffed a trick to him, and even in his weakened condition, he called them on it. He was always a square shooter and demanded fair play.

Nearing his final hours, Cody told his family to let the Elks and Masons handle his funeral arrangements. Then he asked to be baptized. On the afternoon of January 9, Father Christopher V. Walsh arrived at the Decker home at 2932 Lafayette Street to perform the ceremony.

At 12:05 p.m. on January 10, 1916, William Frederick "Buffalo Bill" Cody died. Within the hour, Joseph Bona of the Olinger Mortuary arrived. Bona embalmed Cody's body in the bedroom where he died. Bona later said that due to Cody's large veins, he was able to complete the embalming process in two hours. When he was finished, Bona moved Cody's body to the mortuary. When news of Cody's death was made public, telegrams of condolence came in from all over the world and across the country. Among those sent by President Woodrow Wilson and General Nelson Miles was a joint message of sympathy from Oglala Lakota chief Jack Red Cloud and his band.

On January 14, 1916, Cody's flag-draped coffin lay in the rotunda of the Colorado State Capitol. Over twenty thousand mourners filed past the casket to pay their respects. Cody's casket was then placed on a caisson as the Denver Elks Lodge No. 17 led the funeral procession through the streets of downtown Denver to the Elks Lodge, where the funeral was held. Following the funeral, Cody's body was returned to the Olinger Mortuary, where it would stay for five long months.

When it was announced that Cody would be buried atop Lookout Mountain above Golden, Colorado, several dignitaries and citizens of Cody, Wyoming, protested and even challenged the decision in court. The Cody, Wyoming contingent produced a will drawn up by Cody in 1906, in which he requested to be buried on Cedar Mountain, above the town of Cody. However, the Cody family produced a subsequent will that was signed and executed on February 19, 1913, in North Platte, Nebraska. While that will revoked all previous wills, Cody stipulated that his entire estate would go to his wife, Louisa, who was also named executor.

In the meantime, the William F. Cody Memorial Association, created to ensure a proper burial and memorial, made several trips to Lookout Mountain. Finally, by mid-May, a suitable spot had been agreed upon by the Cody family. The grave site was completed, and the burial took place on June 3, 1917. The casket was transported up the hill from Denver. Along with the Cody family, members of the Grand Army of the Republic were present, as well as several thousand mourners. The Golden City Masonic Lodge performed the burial ceremony, during which family and close friends were allowed one last look at Cody. A few years later, the vice-president of the William F. Cody Memorial Association Theodore Roosevelt observed:

> *It seems to me peculiarly appropriate to erect the monument on a lofty perch like Lookout Mountain, the neighborhood of which to the city of Denver renders it easy as access for all our people—for Buffalo Bill was an American of all Americans.*

On October 26, 1918, the City and County of Denver placed a bronze commemorative plaque over Cody's grave "to remain until after the war and the Cody memorial is erected." Three years later, on October 21, 1921, Louisa Cody, who had died the previous day, was buried beside her husband. Following Cody's death, his foster son, Johnny Baker, came into possession of many of Cody's personal items. Baker had a vision to create a lasting memorial to the great frontier showman. In 1920, Baker wrote a letter to the City of Denver, outlining his idea:

> *I have a collection which would be of great interest to the visitors to Lookout Mountain, and if it's possible to get a location adjacent to his tomb, I would erect a building to conform to the architecture of the mountain park's theme.*[77]

To honor the life and legend of Buffalo Bill, in September 1921, Baker opened the Pahaska Tepee in honor of Cody's Lakota name in conjunction with the City and County of Denver. Located just below the site of Cody's grave, the facility housed the exhibits of Cody's possessions. When Louisa Cody died, Baker acquired many of her personal items and correspondence.

The Pahaska Tepee Museum opened to the pubic on Memorial Day weekend 1921. The nucleus of the museum were many artifacts of Cody's *Wild West Show*, as well as his personal possessions. Among the many items were Cody's silver-mounted saddles, bridles and guns. Cody's clothing, including his show jackets and buckskins that he wore during performances, boots, gloves and hats were all on display. Baker also had the last cartridge Cody fired from a gun, the coin he hit with that shot, the head of the last buffalo Cody shot, as well as a lock of Cody's hair and the receipt of the last money Buffalo Bill had earned with his show. These possessions, along with the hat that Buffalo Bill had worn at his last public appearance in Glenwood

Buffalo Bill Cody is buried on top of Lookout Mountain near Golden, Colorado. *Buffalo Bill Museum.*

Springs on November 11, 1916, all became the showcase of Baker's tribute to the legendary life of Buffalo Bill Cody. For years, the scalp of Yellow Hair was on display at the original Pahaska Tepee. According to Steve Friesen, the director of the Buffalo Bill Museum, this particular display is now in Cody, Wyoming; however, relics and maps of the event are on display at Pahaska Tepee Museum. The original Pahaska Tepee Museum collection has grown over the years, as more items related to Cody's life have been discovered. Today, the Buffalo Bill Museum offers a unique array of extraordinary exhibits related to the life of Buffalo Bill Cody.

William F. "Buffalo Bill" Cody epitomized the frontier spirit of the West. His legend will always be synonymous with the frontier he helped promote and keep alive just a bit longer.

NOTES

Chapter 1

1. Lavender, *Bent's Fort*, 48–49.
2. Drumm, *Down the Santa Fe Trail*, 61.
3. Lavender, *Bent's Fort*, 286.
4. "Insurrection in Taos," *New Mexico Magazine*.
5. The body of Robert Bent was later reinterred in Saint Louis, Missouri.
6. Lavender, *Bent's Fort*, 366.
7. Wommack, "Tragedy at Sand Creek."

Chapter 2

8. Hafen, "Fort Davy Crockett."
9. Ibid.

Chapter 3

10. The area was named for Daniel Boone, who arrived in 1799, and the salt licks in the region.
11. Interview with Christopher "Kit" Carson III.
12. Simmons, *Carson & His Three Wives*, 26.
13. Ibid., 72.
14. "Insurrection in Taos," *New Mexico Magazine*.
15. The body of Robert Bent was later reinterred in Saint Louis, Missouri.
16. Sabin, *Kit Carson Days*, 2:783.
17. Simmons, *Carson & His Three Wives*, 80.
18. Josefa's marker in the Taos Cemetery incorrectly gives his date of death as April 23.

Chapter 4

19. Murray, *Citadel on the Santa Fe Trail*, 12.
20. Howbert, *Memories of a Lifetime*, 121.
21. Wommack, "Tragedy at Sand Creek."
22. Murray, *Citadel on the Santa Fe Trail*, 20.

Chapter 5

23. Jessen, "Papa's Cabin Lost."
24. Gates, *Mariano Medina*, 18.
25. Jessen, "Medina Built a Fort."

Chapter 6

26. Hewett, "Tom Tobin." Hewett would go on to write several books regarding the Colorado frontier, including *Campfire and Trail*, *Pueblo Indian World*, *Indians of the Rio Grande Valley* and *Kit Carson: He Led the Way*.
27. Price, *Season of Terror*, 243.
28. History of Fort Garland; also see, Wommack, "Fort Garland."
29. Perkins, *Tom Tobin*, 80.
30. Price, *Season of Terror*, 150.
31. Ibid., 199.
32. Perkins, *Tom Tobin*, 159.
33. Tobin's Hawken rifle is on display at the Abbey Museum in Canon City, Colorado.
34. "Capture of the Espinosas," *Colorado Magazine*.
35. Price, *Season of Terror*, 257.
36. "Capture of the Espinosas," *Colorado Magazine*.
37. Ibid.
38. Colorado History Center Archives.
39. Ibid.
40. Hewett, "Tom Tobin."
41. Perkins, *Tom Tobin*, 230.
42. Wommack, "From the Grave."
43. Perkins, *Tom Tobin*, 231.
44. Colorado History Center, Carl Wulsten statement, manuscript collection.
45. Perkins, *Tom Tobin*, 238.
46. The cemetery is now located on private land owned by the Malcolm Forbes estate. Permission to enter must be obtained at the gate entrance. There is a marker to both Tom and Maria located there; however, Maria's marker is broken in half.
47. Hewett, "Tom Tobin."

Chapter 7

48. History of Fort Garland, 26.
49. Ibid., 29.

Chapter 8

50. The year 1798 is the one most historians use as Beckwourth's birth year; however, biographer Elinor Wilson makes a credible argument for the year 1800 in her work *Jim Beckwourth*.
51. History of Fort Garland.
52. Lavender, *Bent's Fort*, 367.

Chapter 11

53. Hyde, *Life of George Bent*, 83.
54. Wommack, "Mo-chi." Wild West magazine, April 2004.
55. William M. Hudnut's testimony before the First Judicial Court of Colorado Territory, November 23, 1866. Also see, Parkhill, *Law Goes West*, 48.
56. Ibid.
57. Hyde, *Life of George Bent*, 171.
58. The local Julesburg paper the *Grit-Advocate*, October 21, 1920.
59. Hyde, *Life of George Bent*, 182–83.
60. Halaas, "All the Camp Was Weeping." Also see Halaas and Masich, *Halfbreed*, 211.

Chapter 12

61. Hyde, *Life of George Bent*, 169.
62. Dunn, *Indian Vengeance at Julesburg*, 7.
63. John L. Sipes, the great-grandson of Mo-chi and Medicine Water and a Cheyenne tribal historian. Documents, records and correspondence are now in the possession of the author.
64. Wommack, "From the Grave."

Chapter 13

65. Cody, *Life of Hon. William F. Cody*, 48. All quotes from Cody are attributed to this source unless otherwise noted.
66. Friesen, *Buffalo Bill*, 7.
67. Eugene Carr, Report to General G.D. Ruggles, received 1869; also see, Broome, *Dog Soldier Justice*, 75.
68. Ibid.

69. Carr, "Reminiscences," 15–16.
70. Hyde, *Life of George Bent*, 332.
71. Christian Madsen Papers, Buffalo Bill Museum archives, courtesy of Steve Friesen.
72. Friesen, *Buffalo Bill*, 49.
73. Yost, *Buffalo Bill*, 262.
74. Friesen, *Buffalo Bill*, 103.
75. Buffalo Bill Museum archives, courtesy of Steve Friesen.
76. Fowler, *Timber Line*, 317.
77. Steve Friesen, director of the Buffalo Bill Museum and Archives.

BIBLIOGRAPHY

Interviews and Correspondence

Christopher "Kit" Carson III

Government Publications

Annual Report of the Commissioner of Indian Affairs. 1859.
Carr, Eugene. Report to General G.D. Ruggles. Received 1869.
Report of the Commissioners of Indian Affairs For the Year 1866. Washington D.C.
Report on Indian Affairs by the Acting Commissioner for the Year 1868. Washington D.C.
United States Congress, House of Representatives. "The Chivington Massacre." Report of the Joint Special Committee. Appointed Under Resolution of March 3, 1865.
United States Congress, House of Representatives. Joint Committee on the Conduct of War. 38th Congress. Washington, D.C., 1865.
United States Department of the Interior, Bureau of Indian Affairs. Annual Report. 1865.
United States Department of the Interior, Bureau of Indian Affairs. Annual Report. 1916.
The War of the Rebellion: A Compilation of the Official Records of the Union and Confederate Armies.

State and Federal Documental Archives and Sources

Company Muster Roll of July 29–August 31, 1861. Transcripts of the Colorado volunteers records. State of Colorado, Division of the Archives and Public Records.
Department of the Interior, Indian Field Office. Concho, OK. 1928.
Department of the Interior, Seger Indian Agency. Census Records. Colony, OK.

Unpublished Works and Manuscripts

Berthrong, Donald J., and John L. Sipes. Cheyenne and Arapaho Collections, Land Allotment Files and Cheyenne Prisoner Files.

Carr, Eugene. "Reminiscences."

Hemphill, Anne E. Collection, Silas Soule and Hersa Coberly Soule Letters. Byron Strom, custodian.

Sipes, John L. Cheyenne Files, Tribal Historian, Cheyenne Nation. Now in the possession of Linda Wommack.

Wynkoop, Edward W. "Unfinished Colorado History, 1886." Colorado History Center, MSS II-20.

Newspapers

The various local newspaper archives accessed for this work are noted in the exact quotes used throughout the text.

Historical Archives and Resources

Chavez History Library. Palace of the Governors, Santa Fe, New Mexico. Angelico Fray Collection.

Oklahoma Historical Society. Letter to Miles. George Bent File, Indian Archives.

Sublett County Historical Society. "The Fur Trade and Rendezvous of the Green River Valley." Museum of the Mountain Man. 2005.

Colorado College

Buffalo Bill Museum Archives. Courtesy of Steve Friesen.

Christian Madsen Papers.

Colorado History Center. Carl Wulsten statement. Manuscription collection.

————. Early Far West Notebooks. Francis W. Cragin Collection.

George Bent letters to George E. Hyde.

Hafen, Leroy R. "Fort Davy Crockett, Its Fur Men and Visitors." *Colorado Magazine* no. 29 (September 1962).

History of Fort Garland Museum. 2005.

John Evans Collection. Indian Affairs ledger book.

John Evans personal correspondence. First Regiment of Colorado Volunteer Records and Company Muster Roll.

Sanford, A.B. "Reminiscences of Kit Carson, Jr." *Colorado Magazine* (July 1948).

Tutt Library Collections.

United States Military. Commission reports at Camp Weld.

William N. Byers Papers.

Wynkoop, Edward W. Unfinished manuscript, MSS II.

Denver Public Library Western History Collection

E.S. Ricker Papers.
F.W. Cragin Papers.
George Bent Letters.
Photographs courtesy of Coi Gerhig, DPL photograph editor.
Rocky Mountain News Archives.
Silas Soule Papers, MSS 982.
Thayer, William M. *Marvels of the New West.* N.p.: Henry Bill Publishing Company, 1886. Courtesy, Denver Public Libray. Western History Reseach Room.

Fort Collins Museum of Local History.

Fort Garland Museum.Fort Garland Colorado History Center.
Sterling, Colorado Museum of Local History.

Periodicals and Historical Journals

Ashley, Susan Riley. "Reminiscences of Colorado in the Early 'Sixties.'" *Colorado Magazine* 13 (1936): 219–30.
"The Capture of the Espinosas." *Colorado Magazine* (1932).
Cobb, Frank. M. "The Lawrence Part of Pike's Peakers and the Founding of St. Charles." *Colorado Magazine* (September 1933): 194–97.
Cobern, W.S. "Raid Up the Platte." In *True History of Some of the Pioneers of Colorado.* N.p.: Cobern, Patterson and Shaw, 1909.
Halaas, David. "All the Camp Was Weeping, George Bent and the Sand Creek Massacre." *Colorado Heritage Magazine* (summer 1995).
Hewett, Edgar L. "Tom Tobin." *Colorado Magazine,* September 1946.
"Insurrection in Taos." *New Mexico Magazine,* April 1942.
Jessen, Kenneth. "Louis Papa's Cabin Lost." *Reporter-Herald,* November 28, 2015.
———. "Spanish-Speaking Mariano Medina Built a Fort." *Reporter-Herald,* July 26, 2014.
Kraft, Louis. "When Wynkoop Was Sheriff." *Wild West Magazine,* April 2011.
Milavec, Pam. "Alias Emma S. Soule: Corrected Historical Fictions Surrounding Silas Soule and the Sand Creek Massacre." *Denver Westerners Roundup* (July–August 2005).
Perkins, LaVonne. "Silas Soule, His Widow Heresa [*sic*], and the Rest of the Story." *Denver Westerners Roundup* (March–April 1999).
Prentice, C.A. "Captain Silas S. Soule, a Pioneer Martyr." *Colorado Magazine* (November–December 1935).
Sayre, Hal. "Early Central City Theatrical and Other Reminiscences." *Colorado Magazine* 6 (1929): 47–53.
Wommack, Linda. "Fort Garland." *Wild West Magazine,* February 2013.
———. "In the Eye of the Storm: The Sand Creek Massacre." *True West Magazine,* November 2003.

————. "Mo-chi: The First Female Cheyenne Warrior." *Wild West Magazine*, 2008.

————. "Tragedy at Sand Creek." *True West Magazine*, September, 2003.

Books

Berthrong, Donald J. *The Cheyenne and Arapaho Ordeal: Reservation and Agency Life in the Indian Territory, 1875–1907*. Norman: University of Oklahoma Press, 1976.

————. *The Southern Cheyennes*. Norman: University of Oklahoma Press, 1963.

Bonner, T.D. *Life and Adventures of James P. Beckwourth: Mounteer, Scout, and Pioneer and Chief of the Crow Nation of Indians, Written from His Own Dictation*. New York: Harper & Brothers, 1856.

Broome, Jeff. *Dog Soldier Justice*. Englewood, CO: Aberdeen Books, 2013.

Cody, William F. *The Life of Hon. William F. Cody, Known as Buffalo Bill the Famous Hunter, Scout and Guide*. Lincoln: University of Nebraska Press, 1978. First printed in 1879.

Craig, Reginald S. *The Fighting Parson*. N.p.: Westernlore Press, 1959.

Custer, George Armstrong. *My Life on the Plains*. New York: Promontory Press, 1995. First printed in 1874.

Drumm, Stella M. *Down the Santa Fe Trail and Into New Mexico: The Diary of Susan Shelby Magoffin*. Lincoln: Bison Books, 1982.

Dunlay, Thomas W. *Kit Carson and the Indians*. Lincoln: University of Nebraska Press, 2005.

Dunn, Ruth. *Indian Vengence at Julesburg*. N.p.: Self-published, 1972.

Dunn, William R. (lieutenant colonel). *I Stand By Sand Creek: A Defense of Colonel John M. Chivington and the Third Colorado Cavalry*. Johnstown, CO: Old Army Press, 1985.

Fowler, Gene. *Timber Line*. New York: Comstock Book Distributors, 1933.

Frazer, Robert W. *Forts of the West*. Norman: University of Oklahoma Press, 1972.

Friesen, Steve. *Buffalo Bill: Scout, Showman, Visionary*. Denver, CO: Fulcrum Publications, 2010.

Gates, Zethyl. *Mariano Medina: Colorado Mountain Man*. Chicago: Johnson Publishing Company, 1981.

Greene, Jerome A. *Washita: The U.S. Army and the Southern Cheyennes, 1867–1869*. Norman: University of Oklahoma Press, 2004.

Greene, Jerome A., and Douglas D. Scott. *Finding Sand Creek: History, Archeology, and the 1864 Massacre Site*. Norman: University of Oklahoma Press, 2004.

Grinnell, George Bird. *The Cheyenne Indians*. Vols. 1 and 2. Lincoln: University of Nebraska Press, 1923.

————. *The Fighting Cheyennes*. New York: C. Scribner's Sons, 1915. Reprint, Norman: University of Oklahoma Press, 1956.

Halaas, David F., and Andrew E. Masich. *Halfbreed: The Remarkable True Story of George Bent*. Cambridge, MA: Da Capo Press, 2004.

Hatch, Thom. *Black Kettle: The Cheyenne Chief Who Sought Peace but Found War*. New York: John Wiley & Sons Inc., 2004.

Howbert, Irving. *Memories of a Lifetime in the Pike's Peak Region*. New York: G.P. Putnam's & Sons, 1925.

Hyde, George E. *Life of George Bent: Written from His Letters*. Norman: University of Oklahoma Press, 1968.

Kelly, Lawrence C. *Navajo Roundup*. Boulder, CO: Pruett Publishing, 1970.

Lamm, Richard D., and Duane A. Smith. *Pioneers & Politicians, 10 Colorado Governors in Profile*. Boulder, CO: Pruett Publishing, 1984.

Lavender, Davis. *Bent's Fort*. Lincoln: University of Nebraska Press, 1954.

Leckie, William H. *The Military Conquest of the Southern Plains*. Norman: University of Oklahoma Press, 1963.

Lookingbill, Brad D. *War Dance at Fort Marion*. Norman: University of Oklahoma Press, 2006.

Murray, Robert A. *Citadel on the Santa Fe Trail: The Saga of Bent's Fort*. Johnstown, CO: Old Army Press, 1970.

Nevins, Allan. *Polk: The Diary of a President*. London: Longmans, Green & Co., 1929.

Parkhill, Forbes. *The Law Goes West*. Denver, CO: Sage Books, 1956.

Perkins, James E. *Tom Tobin, Frontiersman*. N.p.: Herodotus Press, 1999.

Pratt, Richard Henry. *Battlefield and Classroom: Four Decades with the American Indian, 1867–1904*. New Haven, CT: Yale University Press, 1964.

Price, Charles. *Season of Terror, the Espinosas in Central Colorado*. Boulder, CO: University Press of Colorado, 2013.

Pritzker, Barry M. *A Native American Encyclopedia: History, Culture, and Peoples*. Oxford, UK: Oxford University Press, 2000.

Propst, Nell Brown. *Forgotton People*. Boulder, CO: Pruett Publishers, 1979.

Prucha, Francis Paul. *The Great White Father: The United States Government and the American Indians*. Lincoln: University of Nebraska Press, 1984.

Quaife, Milo Milton, ed. *Kit Carson's Autobiography*. Lincoln: University of Nebraska Press, 1966. From the original 1935 publication.

Reinfeld, Fred. *Pony Express*. Lincoln: University of Nebraska Press, 1966.

Remley, David. *Kit Carson: The Life of an American Border Man*. Norman: University of Oklahoma Press, 2011.

Roberts, Gary L. *Sand Creek, Tragedy and Symbol*. Norman: University of Oklahoma Press, 1984.

Roberts, Gary L., and David F. Halass. *Written in Blood: The Soule-Cramer Sand Creek Massacre Letters*. Reprint, Los Angeles: Fulcrum Press, 2004.

Sabin, Edwin L. *Kit Carson Days*. 2 vols. N.p.: Press of Pioneers, 1935.

Scott, Bob. *Tom Tobin and the Bloody Espinosas*. Frederick, MD: Publish America, 2004.

Simmons, Marc. *Kit Carson & His Three Wives*. Albuquerque: University of New Mexico Press, 2003.

Utley, Robert M. *The Indian Frontier of the American West 1846–1890*. Lincoln: University of Nebraska Press, 1984.

Ware, Eugene F. *The Indian Wars of 1864*. N.p.: Crane & Company, 1911. Reprint, New York: St. Martin's Press, 1960.

Whiteley, Lee. *The Cherokee Trail, Bent's Old Fort to Fort Bridger*. Denver, CO: Johnson Books, 1999.

Wilson, Elinor. *Jim Beckwourth: Black Mountain Man, War Chief of the Crows, Trader, Trapper, Explorer, Frontiersman, Guide, Scout, Interpreter, Adventurer and Gaudy Liar.* Norman: University of Oklahoma Press, 1972.

Wommack, Linda. *From the Grave: A Roadside Guide to Colorado's Pioneer Cemeteries.* Caldwell, ID: Caxton Press, 1998.

Yost, Nellie Snyder. *Buffalo Bill: His Family, Friends, Fame, Failures, and Fortunes.* Athens, OH: Swallow Press, 1979.

ABOUT THE AUTHOR

A Colorado native, Linda Wommack is a Colorado historian and historical consultant. An award-winning writer, she has written eighteen books on Colorado history, including *Murder in the Mile High City*; *Colorado's Landmark Hotels*; *From the Grave: A Roadside Guide to Colorado's Pioneer Cemeteries*; *Our Ladies of the Tenderloin: Colorado's Legends in Lace*; *Colorado History for Kids: Colorado's Historic Mansions and Castles*; *Colorado's Historic Schools*; *Ann Bassett: Colorado's Cattle Queen*; *Haunted History of Cripple Creek and Teller County*; *Growing Up with the Wild Bunch*; *Ranching Women of Colorado*; *Cripple Creek, Bob Womack and the Greatest Gold Camp on Earth*; and *From Sand Creek to Summit Springs: Colorado's Indian Wars*. She has also contributed to two anthologies concerning western Americana. She is a three-time winner of the prestigious Will Rogers Medallion Award.

Linda has been a contributing editor for *True West Magazine* since 1995 and has been a staff writer for *Wild West Magazine*, contributing a monthly article since 2004. She has written for the *Tombstone Epitaph*, the nation's oldest continuously published newspaper, since 1993. Linda also writes for several publications throughout her state and has won two awards for her work.

Linda's research has been used in several documentary accounts for the national Wild West History Association, historical treatises of the Sand Creek Massacre and as critical historic aspects for the Lawman & Outlaw Museum, as well as the Heritage Center, both in Cripple Creek, Colorado.

Linda feeds her passion for history by participating in activities in many local, state and national preservation projects; attending historical venues and speaking engagements; hosting tours; and becoming involved in historical tours across the state.

She is a member of both the state and national Cemetery Preservation Associations, the Gilpin County Historical Society and the national Wild West History Association, and she is an honorary lifetime member of the Pikes Peak Heritage Society. As a member of Women Writing the West (WWW), Linda has organized quarterly meetings for Colorado members of the WWW for the past ten years, served on the 2014 and 2020 WWW conference steering committees and recently concluded her term as a board member. Linda is the chair for the Women Writing the West DOWNING Journalism Award, an award category she created for the organization in 2017.

Linda has received numerous awards for her writing. She is a three-time recipient of the Will Rogers Medallion Award and has received a best biography award for *Ann Bassett* and *Growing Up With the Wild Bunch* and a best nonfiction award for *Ranching Women of Colorado*. She has received the Six-Shooter Award twice for her magazine articles "Confidentially Told in Brown's Park" and "In the Shadow of Tom Horn."